SERVING TWO MASTERS

By the same author:

Gadfly for God: A History of the Church Times, Hodder & Stoughton, 1991

High and Mitred: Prime Ministers as Bishop-Makers, SPCK, 1992

Reverend Rebels: Five Victorian Clerics and their Fight Against Authority, Darton, Longman & Todd, 1993

Men of Habit: The Franciscan Ideal in Action, Canterbury Press, 1994

A Class of Their Own: Six Public School Headmasters Who Became Archbishop of Canterbury, The Book Guild, 1997

Imperial Vineyard: The Anglican Church in India under the Raj from the Mutiny to Partition, The Book Guild, 1999

SERVING TWO MASTERS

Parish Patronage in the Church of England Since 1714

Bernard Palmer

Foreword by Dr Richard Harries,
Bishop of Oxford

The Book Guild Ltd
Sussex, England

First published in Great Britain in 2003 by
The Book Guild Ltd
25 High Street
Lewes, East Sussex
BN7 2LU

Typesetting in Times by
Acorn Bookwork, Salisbury, Wiltshire

Printed in Great Britain by
Antony Rowe Ltd, Chippenham, Wiltshire

A catalogue record for this book is available from
The British Library.

ISBN 1 85776 776 4

CONTENTS

FOREWORD BY RICHARD HARRIES, BISHOP OF OXFORD

The parson in Evelyn Waugh's novel *A Handful of Dust*, described as 'The Revd Tendril', had been a padre in India. He had obtained his present parish because 'Tony's father had given him the living at the instance of his dentist'. That was only a mildly harmful form of patronage – Tendril continued to preach exactly the same sermons as he had done in the garrison chapel in India: sometimes its exercise has been more sinister, and certainly both more political and mercenary.

This is a pioneering study of a fascinating subject in which political power, ecclesiastical fawning and human greed – as well as a desire to serve the Good Lord – come together in the persons of clerics who are anxiously seeking positions and patrons who enjoy the delicious feeling of exercising patronage. Bernard Palmer's highly readable history, full of anecdotes and memorable quotations, shows the patronage system at its worst: and also how it has been reformed in recent years to make it serve a more democratic Church.

Thomas Hobbes said that liberty is power cut up into little pieces. On that basis the Church of England, with its highly fragmented system of patronage, is Liberty Hall indeed. Its system of dispersed patronage has saved the Church from the tyranny of bishops. Now, as a result of the 1986 Patronage (Benefices) Measure, there is, in principle, a nicely balanced inter-play of patron, parish representatives and bishops. It works well if the patron, whether a college, an individual, a trust or the bishop himself, involves all those responsible from the first, including the shortlisting and certainly the interview process. It's a sign of failure if the parish representatives have to exercise their veto and reject a candidate put forward by the patron. In my experience when the system has worked badly it has been because the patron has tried to act independently of the parish representatives and bishop, or has only brought them into the process after the shortlisting. Where it works well, as it mostly does now, it is another example of the Church of England evolving, gradually adapting anachronistic systems to modern conditions in a way which keeps a fair balance between the parties involved. This book with its vignettes of past ages, at once shocking and amusing, indicates just how far the Church of England has travelled in 300 years.

PREFACE

This book on the bizarre system under which parish priests in the Church of England are appointed covers a period of almost 300 years. It therefore deals necessarily more with the general than with the particular. Nevertheless, it includes plenty of colourful material concerning individual clerics who, for one reason or another, illustrate the quirks of the patronage system as it operated until comparatively recent times.

And those quirks make fascinating reading. Among the issues dealt with in the earlier section of the book are the shameless way in which politicians manipulated parish appointments to suit the interests of their own party; the equally shameless way in which patrons of all sorts, from archbishops and dukes to humble country squires, appointed their friends and relatives to plum livings in the Church; the 'market in souls' which flourished in the eighteenth and nineteenth centuries as advowsons (the right of presentation to a living) were bought and sold as items of property; the relationships, often absurdly obsequious but sometimes stormy, which grew up between parish priests and the lay patrons who had appointed them; and the scandals of plurality and non-residence.

The book concludes with an account of how the whole extra-ordinary system of appointing incumbents in the Church of England was gradually reformed over the course of a century and a half – at first in Parliament, and then in the Church Assembly and General Synod. The battle for reform was long and bitter. The notion that the right to appoint a parish priest was an item of property with a market value of its own proved hard to dislodge, and many Bills came to grief in the Lords or in the Commons. Gradually, however, the reformers had their way, and the iniquities and absurdities of the old system faded from the scene.

Private patrons are still fairly thick on the ground, but their rights and privileges are but a shadow of what they once were. In contrast, diocesan bishops are now all-powerful in securing the appointment of those whom they conceive to be the right men (and, since 1993, women) to parishes – and some critics would no doubt contend that bishops are no better than lay patrons. But at least in most cases parochial church councils now have the power of veto, so can escape being saddled with a hopelessly unsuitable rector or vicar. The closing chapter of my book, based partly on an appeal in the *Church Times* for background information, records a number of recent cases presenting unusual features.

Much of the information contained in *Serving Two Masters* is already available in published form. But it is scattered about in scores of volumes of different kinds (e.g., church history books, biographies, diaries, memoirs, etc.) and is therefore not readily accessible. My book aims to bring all this information together under one cover – which will, hopefully, make it a work of value to professionals in the field as well as one of considerable interest to the general reader, not least through the inclusion of much colourful detail. The closing chapter brings the story right up to date and so ensures that the book is fully relevant to the present day.

Bernard Palmer
Charminster, Dorset

ACKNOWLEDGEMENTS

In compiling this book I have made extensive use of existing church histories, biographies, diaries and memoirs. A full list of these can be found in the bibliography at the end of the volume. I accordingly acknowledge my deep debt to those many authors of whose labours I have made free; and, not least, to the London Library, that invaluable storehouse of literary treasure-trove, where I was able to track down the majority of them.

In particular I must thank Oxford University Press for kindly permitting me to quote extracts from *The Journal of the Rev. William Bagshaw Stevens*, edited by Georgina Galbraith (1965); and SPCK for granting me a like favour in respect of *The Diaries of Thomas Wilson, D.D.*, edited by C.L.S. Linnell (1964).

I am also grateful to those, both individuals and society representatives, who so kindly replied to an appeal for information I made in the *Church Times*. Their response greatly facilitated the writing of my final chapter. And a special word of thanks is due to Mrs Yolande Clarke, formerly of the *Church Times* editorial staff, for her invaluable help in photocopying reports of relevant debates in the General Synod.

Last but not least, I thank my wife for once again transforming my messy transcript into an impeccable fair copy for the publishers; for her much-needed encouragement along the way; and for providing me with the idea for the book, its title, and indeed just about everything else except the actual writing of the book.

B.P.

1

Friends in High Places

'Getting patronage', according to one of the characters in Shaw's *Captain Brassbound's Conversion*, 'is the whole art of life. A man cannot have a career without it'.[1] Many of the clergy in eighteenth- and nineteenth-century England must sadly have come to the same conclusion. If a priest with a jot of ambition in him wanted to end his active ministry in a more rewarding corner of the Lord's vineyard than that in which he had begun it, he needed a friend or friends in high places. That was a fact of ecclesiastical life as it was then lived.

For ecclesiastical purposes the whole of England was (as it still is) divided into geographical parishes, each parish being in the charge of an incumbent (rector, vicar or perpetual curate).* And every incumbent was presented to his 'living' (as a parish was also called, from the fact of its providing its priest with an income on which to live) by a patron. He was 'presented' rather than formally appointed by the patron, in that the bishop of the diocese had first to approve his nomination. This was a technical safeguard which was more illusory than real. A bishop would rarely exercise his right to refuse to accept a patron's nominee, however undesirable he might privately consider him to be. Neither age nor infirmity nor moral misdemeanour was sufficient ground in itself for rejecting a candidate. And, if a bishop *did* pluck up his courage and decline to accept a nomination, there was a real risk that his action

* See note on page 8.

1

would be successfully challenged at law. Even as late as the second half of the nineteenth century bishops were sometimes compelled to institute men who were totally unfit for the parishes concerned. The fact that a clergyman was a paralytic, a drunkard or too old to exercise an adequate ministry was neither here nor there as far as the law was concerned.

Patrons were of various kinds. The precise proportions varied over the years, but at the beginning of the nineteenth century about 10 per cent of parish patronage belonged to the Crown and its various officers such as the Lord Chancellor, 12 per cent to the bishops, 10 per cent to deans and chapters of cathedrals, 7 per cent to Oxford and Cambridge Universities and their constituent colleges, and almost all the remainder to private individuals ranging from dukes to humble country squires.

Crown livings were the subject of much wheeling and dealing on the part of politicians. Although nominally bestowed by the monarch, they were in practice in the gift of the Prime Minister or the Lord Chancellor, who would find themselves besieged by importunate suitors for even the humblest country benefice. So, to secure a Crown living, an applicant needed to have his ear to the political ground. This might also be true in the case of livings in the gift of private individuals, especially if the patron happened to be a grandee who required his nominees to be of the same political persuasion as himself. But even humbler lay patrons often made the same stipulation. In the case of deans and chapters, the filling of vacant livings would be decided either after informal discussion among their members or on a formal majority vote. A vacant college living would normally be awarded to the most senior fellow, though in some cases (as with Parson Woodforde) there would be an election. Every class of patron was subject to the calls of nepotism. This was especially true in the case of peers and bishops, who liked nothing better than to dish out the most valuable livings in their gift to friends and relatives. The most flagrant abuses of the patronage system will be examined in subsequent chapters.

* * * * * * * * * *

The origins of the system are rooted deep in history. From Anglo-Saxon times onwards local lords of the manor had founded churches on their estates, endowing them with an income and reserving to themselves and their heirs the right to present a fit person to the bishop for institution as parish priest. This right of presentation was known as an 'advowson' (from the Latin word *advocatio*: cf. 'advocate'). Monasteries acquired the same right to present priests to livings; and, when they were dissolved at the time of the Reformation, the right passed in many cases to the inheritors of their manors.

Over the centuries the links between the lordship of a manor and the patronage of its church – between squire and parish – sometimes became less close. The advowson of a living might be severed from the local landowner and go outside the parish. Eventually a trade in advowsons grew up under which they were bought and sold like pieces of commercial property. By the middle years of the nineteenth century the trade had become a scandal. The patron might have little or no interest in the welfare of his parishioners and would regard his possession of the advowson as no more than a profitable investment. Hence the frequent nineteenth-century complaint of souls being 'for sale'.

Such a notion, of course, was officially anathema in the Church, being tied up with the sin of simony. This term was derived from the reprehensible actions of Simon Magus described in Acts viii, 18–24, and referred to the purchase or sale of spiritual things such as holy orders. In the Middle Ages the Church authorities were frequently denouncing practices which could be held to be 'simoniacal', and a number of canons were enacted in an effort to stamp out such practices. One canon, framed in 1075, ruled that 'no one buy or sell orders, or any ecclesiastical office wherein the cure of souls is concerned'. Up till the time of the Reformation simony was held to be a sin of such enormity that only the Pope could absolve anyone found guilty of indulging in it. After the Reformation the rule of Rome no longer applied, so Parliament stepped in where the Pope was unable to tread. A statute passed in 1588 was aimed both at the clergyman indulging in simony through, e.g., some financial irregularity connected with the acquisition of a living and also at the patron who connived in the irregularity. The former, if found guilty, would be deprived of the living; the latter would suffer both a heavy fine and the forfeiture of his patronage to the Crown for that turn. The object of the statute, in the words of Sir Robert Phillimore in 1874, 'was to make that illegal by the law of the land which was sinful by the law of the Church'.[2] The parliamentary statute was reinforced by an ecclesiastical canon, passed in 1604, which required all ordinands and recipients of benefices to swear an oath to the effect that their offices had not been obtained by simoniacal transactions – the precursor of the 'declaration against simony' which was substituted for it in 1865.

But what exactly *was* a 'simoniacal transaction'? Here the law was less clear, and all sorts of anomalies arose. Thus it was not simony to purchase the advowson of a living whose incumbent, to the knowledge of both contracting parties, was on the point of death; but it *was* simony to purchase it once the last breath had left his body. It was not simony for a man to purchase an advowson with a secret stipulation that the vendor should pay him interest on the purchase money until the next vacancy occurred; but it *was* simony to accept a benefice under a promise to pay a small annuity out of its income to the widow of the previous incumbent. No wonder that Bishop Magee of Peterborough should have complained to the House of Lords in 1874 that the difference between what the law allowed and what it forbade was in most cases so purely technical and conventional that it touched no man's conscience: 'Evasions of a law so utterly unreasonable come to be but lightly regarded ... The law of simony has thus, as it were, slipped from off its moral basis and been broken into shapeless fragments in its fall'.[3]

A particularly flagrant case had occurred only thirty years previously. The Dean of York, William Cockburn, had been convicted by an ecclesiastical court in 1841 of selling the next presentations to the livings of which as dean he was patron, and had been sentenced by his archbishop to be deprived of his deanery for simony. On appeal to the secular courts, however, he had had the sentence put aside on the technical ground that the charge against him had been brought under the wrong piece of church legislation. The dean had maintained his innocence throughout the hearings;* he was reinstated, and continued in office until his death in 1858.[4]

The charge in his case had concerned 'next presentations', as they were termed: the sale of the right to nominate a man to a benefice when the current incumbent resigned or died. Such sales had apparently not been foreseen by the parliament of Queen Elizabeth I which had approved the statute of 1588. It was left to a parliament of Queen Anne in 1713 to attempt to remedy the position by passing a further statute. This began by observing that 'some of the clergy have procured preferments for themselves by buying ecclesiastical livings' and then enacting that:

if any person ... shall by reason of any promise, agreement etc. ... take, procure, or accept the next avoidance of, or presentation to, any benefice with cure of souls, dignity or prebend, or

---

* 'If anyone makes enquiries about my private arrangements', he remarked at the time, 'you may tell them that, if I had 100 livings, since the Spoliation Bill was talked of I would have resolved to sell them all'. A successor described him as an 'impossible person, very quarrelsome and, I should think, entirely devoid of scruple'.[5]

living ecclesiastical, and shall be presented or collated there-
upon, every such presentation &c. ... shall be utterly void,
frustrate, and of no effect in law, and such agreement shall be
deemed and taken to be a simoniacal contract.[6]

Unfortunately for the framers of the statute, it left an obvious
loophole for those wishing to evade its behests. A clergyman
was still fully entitled to buy the advowson of the desired living
– i.e., the perpetual presentation – for himself. Then all he had
to do was to present himself to the living and sell the
advowson as soon as he wanted to move again. A lawyer,
writing in 1898, reckoned that as many as 600 benefices in the
gift of the sitting incumbent had been resold in this way within
recent years.[7] It was also possible for a priest to evade the
provisions of the statute by arranging for the purchase of the
next presentation to be made in the name of his wife, who
would then, quite legally, present her husband to the living.
And, if he was unmarried, he could act through some other
relative or middleman.

For most of the period covered by this history more than
half the advowsons of English parishes were owned by private
individuals ranging from peers to minor members of the
gentry. A number of lists exist, both official and unofficial,
analysing the distribution of advowsons among the different
classes of holder.

The first is that compiled by Browne Willis in his *A Survey
of the Cathedrals*, first published in 1742. This analysed the
patronage of 11,866 parishes and chapelries in England and
Wales. Willis found that the Crown was patron of 9.6 per cent
of these; bishops, cathedral chapters and parochial clergymen
of 26.1 per cent; educational foundations of 6.7 per cent;
'parishioners' of 0.8 per cent; private individuals (of whom
about a quarter were peers) of 53.4 per cent; and 'others' of 3.4
per cent. Large holdings of advowsons were uncommon.
Although 38.4 per cent of the 2,993 private patrons in 1742
held at least two advowsons and 22 per cent at least three, only

8 per cent had five or more livings in their gift and only 2.5 per cent (71 individuals) ten or more – though these latter patrons (two out of three of whom were peers) controlled the presentations to nearly 10 per cent of all the livings in the Church of England. The really large advowson-holders were very rare birds indeed. Patrons of thirty livings or more represented a mere one-tenth of 1 per cent of the total number of private patrons. In only ninety-two parishes (0.8 per cent) was the incumbent chosen by the parishioners as a whole or by a town corporation.[8]

Eighty years later the position had not changed substantially. Out of 10,693 livings, according to the census of 1821, the Crown presented to 1,048 (9.8 per cent); the bishops, cathedral chapters and educational foundations to 3,026 (28.3 per cent); and 'private individuals' to 6,619 (61.9 per cent). As the nineteenth century advanced, so did the number of livings, new parishes being created to meet the needs of the rapidly expanding towns and cities. The century saw a substantial increase in episcopal patronage, the number of advowsons held by bishops more than doubling in the period 1821–1901. In the same period the number held by private patrons also increased, though not to anything like the same extent. M.J. Roberts, in an article for the *Journal of Ecclesiastical History*, includes a table showing changes in the distribution of patronage in England and Wales between 1821 and 1901 (the figures for 'others' include cathedral chapters and universities):[9]

Year	Crown	Bishops	Private patrons	Others	Total number of benefices
1821	1,048	1,301	6,619	1,725	10,693
1835	952	1,248	5,096	3,244	10,540
1853	1,144	1,853	6,092	2,639	11,728
1878	1,085	2,659	6,982	2,654	13,380
1901	c.1,020	c.3,030	c.7,350	c.2,650	c.14,050

* * * * * * * * * *

7

It must not be supposed that the overall position regarding patronage was quite as black as is sometimes painted. Not all patrons were hard-hearted, mercenary or concerned only with finding soft berths for their nearest and dearest. Many were genuinely concerned with discovering the right man for the job – even if only too often, the right man *did* turn out to be a friend or relative. Gross abuses of the powers of patronage were relatively uncommon – and hit the contemporary headlines because of their rarity. Even the Duke of Newcastle, for all his reputation as an ecclesiastical manipulator, made it a general rule to give priority to recommendations based on local knowledge. Nevertheless, it cannot be denied that patronage as a whole, in the Church as in other fields, was seen as a means of satisfying legitimate demands. One has only to read the novels of Jane Austen to see how readily her characters reflect her own known views on the claims of kinship in the game of preferment. It may seem shocking nowadays to observe the shameless way in which bishops and peers gave away the numerous livings in their gift to their kith and kin, but they were only reflecting the spirit of their times. Gradually the system came to be regarded for the scandal that it undoubtedly was. But the process of reform was a very gradual one. It had to be fought, in the face of the many defenders of so-called 'private property', every inch of the way.

* * * * * * * * * *

A Note about Incumbents

Incumbents of English parishes belong to one of three classes: rector, vicar and perpetual curate. All of them possess the so-called 'parson's freehold'. This provides them with security of tenure by guaranteeing that they cannot be removed from their benefices unless found guilty of heretical teaching or conduct deemed to be 'unseemly'. This right is being gradually whittled away by the legal device of suspending the presentation of a benefice and appointing a 'priest-in-charge' for a fixed term of years.

The difference between a rector and a vicar was based on the class of tithes which they received as benefice income. Tithes represented the payment of a tenth part of all the produce of parish lands. The 'greater tithes' were the tithes of the major crops such as wheat, oats, etc.; the 'lesser tithes' were the tithes of minor produce such as lambs and chickens.

A *rector* was the incumbent of a parish who received the greater tithes connected with the benefice. A *vicar*, in pre-Reformation days, was a priest appointed by a monastery to look after a parish as its deputy (the Latin word for which was *vicarius*); he received the lesser tithes. A *perpetual curate* was a slightly inferior form of vicar who was likewise appointed by a monastery as its deputy in a parish but who received no tithes at all; but, like rectors and vicars, he had security of tenure – hence his title 'perpetual'.

The Church was compelled, by the Tithe Act of 1936, to surrender its income from tithe payments in exchange for about £70 million of government stock, so the distinction between rectors, vicars and perpetual curates is nowadays academic. In the press and elsewhere they are usually all called 'vicars' – as indeed, increasingly, are Roman Catholic priests and Free Church ministers.

2

God and Caesar

There is a story, probably apocryphal, that a certain clergyman who found himself having to preach before Lord North when he was Prime Minister chose for his biblical text 'Promotion cometh neither from the East, nor from the West, nor yet from the South'.*[1] True or not, the story neatly underlines the way in which in those days, where preferment was concerned, Church and State were intimately linked. The point was pressed home a little later when the younger Pitt, still very young as Prime Ministers went, was to be present at a university sermon in Great St Mary's, Cambridge. It was suggested by one wag that an appropriate text for the occasion (apropos of the multitude of calls on the Premier's bounty) would be: 'There is a lad here which hath five barley loaves and two small fishes, but what are they among so many?'[2]

The eighteenth century was a corrupt age, and clergymen wishing to rise in the Church, or indeed to acquire the 'right sort' of living, needed friends in high places. Many livings were in the gift of the Crown (which meant in effect the Prime Minister or the Lord Chancellor), so those high-placed friends had necessarily to have the ear of politicians and the clerics

---

*It was North who, when questioned about the propriety of appointing his half-brother Brownlow to the bishopric of Coventry and Lichfield at the age of 29, is said to have replied: 'Indeed my brother is no doubt young to be a bishop, but when he is older he will no longer have a brother as Prime Minister'.[3]

themselves to support the correct political party. Sir Robert Walpole, during his long reign as Premier, reserved all his official patronage, down to the humblest parish benefice, exclusively for Whig sympathizers; so, where Crown livings were concerned, they were filled with Whig rectors and vicars. The balance was restored to some extent by the Tory squires, who filled the numerous livings in their gift with Tory incumbents; but in the higher echelons of the Church, including the episcopate, the Whig interest was predominant.

Of course there was a veneer of respectability papering over the crude concept of ecclesiastical jobs for the boys. Clerics under consideration for vacant posts had (in theory at least) to be men of good character and of irreproachable morals. But political reliability was the all-important requirement; and friends of the government in the country, such as justices of the peace, acted as ecclesiastical talent-spotters on the lookout for suitable candidates for preferment. From the government's point of view it was necessary to keep its influential supporters sweet by rewarding them with Crown appointments for their dependants.

This could sometimes lead to embarrassment, as when two government supporters were both angling for the same post for their nominees. Such a tussle occurred in 1748–49 over the living of Buckland Brewer, in Devon, which had fallen vacant. The two protagonists were Lords Rolle and Orford. Rolle wanted the benefice for a brother of his friend Sir Bourchier Wrey; Orford (who was Lord Lieutenant of the county) wanted it for his domestic chaplain. At that time the unofficial 'Minister for Ecclesiastical Affairs' was the Duke of Newcastle (of whom more anon); and it was Newcastle who found himself having to sort out the rival claims.

Rolle and Orford detested each other, Orford going so far as to dub Rolle and Wrey 'dirty, silly fellows'. Rolle reminded Newcastle that he had spent nearly £8,000 in fighting elections at Barnstaple on behalf of the Whigs; Orford threatened to

11

resign his lord-lieutenancy if his chaplain was not awarded the vacant living. He told the Duke bluntly: 'My Lord, the Point is now whether these two Gentlemen [Rolle and Wrey] or myself have the greatest weight with Your Grace and the rest of the Administration'. Just as it seemed as if, for Newcastle, it was a no-win situation, Providence intervened in the shape of a vacancy in the nearby Crown living of Ashburton with St Peter Tavy, so that the spoils could be more or less evenly divided. But it had taken eighteen months of often bitter wrangling to settle the fate of a single insignificant country benefice.[4]

If you were an ambitious cleric in those days it was necessary to be quick off the mark. Quite apart from the fact that your sponsor might have to push your claims against those of a candidate backed by a rival political mandarin, you had to secure a sponsor in the first place. It was therefore essential to have your hat in the ring as soon as possible, even if it meant stationing a 'spy' in the parish to which you aspired who could notify you of the death of its elderly or ailing incumbent. Much energy was expended by clergymen in trying to extract from government ministers the promise of a living before it had actually fallen vacant. Ministers, for their part, were reluctant to make such a pledge in advance: they risked being swamped with similar requests. But their reluctance did little to stem the flow. Edmund Pyle, a country incumbent whose position as chaplain to King George II kept him in touch with Court gossip, was typical of many in advising his friend Samuel Kerrich not to be backward in coming forward: 'Ask, say I, and with importunity too; if you don't, there are those that will'.[5] The extent of the scheming involved in securing a plum living – or indeed a living of any sort – will be examined in depth in chapter five.

Although Crown appointments were theoretically the prerogative of the Prime Minister of the day, the role of the monarch was far from negligible. George II, for instance, caused immense irritation to the Duke of Newcastle, who handled Church affairs either as or for the Premier, by raising constant objections to candidates put forward for preferment. Indeed he seems to have taken a particular delight in keeping the Duke dangling on a hook for weeks at a time before eventually agreeing to his choice of candidate. But George knew his limitations. When John Thomas, the English chaplain at Hamburg, asked him for a prebend, the King explained that it was not in his power to oblige the applicant, as his ministers reserved such plums for their own nominees:

> I will tell you what I will do for you. They do not much mind livings, and I will give you the first living that falls, and then I will make you one of my chaplains, and then the next time I come to Hanover you shall come over with me as my chaplain; and then, if a prebend or deanery should happen to fall, you would have a good chance of succeeding to it; and this is the only way wherein I can procure any such thing for you.[6]

Thomas was rewarded in due course with the rectory of St Vedast, Foster Lane, in the City of London, and a little later with the deanery of Peterborough. This latter appointment caused friction between the King and Newcastle, who had already 'in a manner engaged' it to the Master of St John's College, Cambridge. Newcastle asked Thomas to waive his right to it in exchange for the promise of a better deanery or a canonry of St Paul's when one became vacant. Thomas declined to oblige: 'As the king had been graciously pleased to give him the deanery, he could not with any decency or good manners decline his Majesty's favour; but his grace might vacate the deanery by giving him a better thing as soon as ever he pleased'.[7] Newcastle's opportunity came in 1743, when Thomas was made Bishop of St Asaph. His deanery was thus available to the Duke for bestowal at last on the Master of St John's.

This was one occasion when the King *did* get the better of Newcastle, who usually succeeded in the end but who found his royal master a constant trial. On one occasion he complained to a friend: 'I will put my shoulders to the work, but I doubt the success ... I work hard, I do my best, and we may all be whispered out of our characters'.[8]

It was not only the King who proved a thorn in the Duke's flesh. George's consort, Queen Caroline, could at times be equally obdurate. She played a key role in the disposal of ecclesiastical patronage. Much light on that role is cast by her Mistress of the Robes, Mrs Clayton (afterwards Viscountess Sundon), in her memoirs, which include many letters soliciting her aid in obtaining favours from her royal mistress. The Queen, in the words of the Duchess of Somerset, 'made all the clergy of England happy by taking them under her immediate protection'.[9] And, as access to the Queen could usually be obtained only through the good offices of Mrs Clayton, the latter acquired an influence similar to that enjoyed by the Duchess of Marlborough under Queen Anne.

Her sway extended in many directions. In 1733 we find the Lord Chancellor's wife writing to her: 'Madam ... you may depend upon my Lord's not disposing of the living till he has your orders ... it was one of the livings upon the list you gave me, for which reason I hope it is worth your friend's taking'.[10] And her kinsman, Robert Clayton, Bishop of Killala and Achonry in Ireland, assures her about the same time:

> As I have two Bishoprics, I have likewise another Dean, who is very old, and possesses the best livings that are in my gift; but, though he is ninety years of age, he is very hearty, and may last a good while. However, as he must die sometime or other, I shall take care to inform you of it, if it happens in my time, and will not dispose of the livings which are in my donation till I receive your commands.[11]

The horse-trading carried on between King George II and his prime ministers continued under his successor, George III. In 1781, for instance, the then Prime Minister, Lord North,

14

was able to secure the translation of his half-brother Brownlow from Worcester to Winchester in fulfilment of a promise extracted from the King four years earlier – as a reward for the premier's not pressing Brownlow's claim to the archbishopric of York.*[12]

* * * * * * * * * *

The bishops and other leading clerics in Newcastle's day (and due in no small part to his efforts) might have been Whigs; but the majority of the clergy, especially those in the country, remained Tories at heart. Their career prospects might depend on their endearing themselves to Whig patrons or friends of the Whig government, but many of them were happy to live out their lives unconcerned with the doings of the great world beyond their parishes and to minister to their flocks in rural obscurity. For men of ambition, however, such a life of rustic ease possessed insufficient attractions; and partisan loyalties came into play as they sought their own advancement.

At times such loyalties were crucial. But seeking preferment was often an uphill task, as is made plain in a letter written in 1734 by a Cambridgeshire cleric, Henry Travers, to a fellow clergyman in Kent. His main hopes of securing a suitable appointment, he said, were dependent on 'Party Zeal and the Spirit of Politics'. But, he continued, 'I confess to you that I do not much depend upon [it], having experienced that insatiable Rancour with which the different Parties [in] England prosecute one another; and 'tis plain to me that nothing is to be expected from Either of them unless a Man will give himself up

---

*Brownlow North was Bishop of Winchester for thirty-nine years. His nepotism was notorious even by the standards of the times. When he died in 1820 his body was borne to its resting-place in the cathedral by six prebendaries, all his family connections: two sons, two sons-in-law and two nephews-by-marriage.

entirely to be influenced by their Opinions'.[13] Once a post had been secured, a loyal priest would lose no opportunity of buttering up his patron – like John Gallop, 'clerk of the church' in Hastings, Sussex, on the morrow of a successful parliamentary election:

> My Lord, my humble service to your honour, and at the Request of the freemen, your friends, I shall, the next Lord's day, God willing, perform their desires and my owne in singing the 20th Psalm, the first 4 verses, & the last 4 verses of the 11th psalm – this is the joyfull day indeed, and I am sure a joyfuller day to Hastings, to all people's Satisfaction, hath not been for many years.[14]

* * * * * * * * * *

Mention has been made of the Duke of Newcastle's role in masterminding ecclesiastical appointments. He deserves a closer inspection, if only because of the dominant part he played in the middle years of the eighteenth century in ensuring the entrenchment of the Crown's ecclesiastical patronage in the political system. He soon became recognized as the central clearing-house for appointments. In coordinating the Church's patronage, however, he took pains to ensure that it was exercised in the interests of the Whig Party. As he remarked on one occasion, 'The rule which I have laid down to myself in all recommendations which I have ever made to the Crown has been, first, to recommend None whom I did not think most sincerely well-affected to His Majesty and His Government, and to the Principles upon which it is founded'.[15]

Thomas Pelham-Holles, 1st Duke of Newcastle (1693–1768) was a genuinely devout man who attended church service twice a day whenever possible and who performed many charitable acts. He was also a man of blameless private life and personally incorruptible. There are many proofs of his piety such as his correspondence with Bishop Hume of Oxford about prayers and preparation for Holy Communion. It is

16

therefore paradoxical, but typical of the period in which he lived, that such a man of personal integrity should have exercised such blatant political partiality in bestowing the appointments within his gift. As Bishop Thomas Newton of Bristol cynically commented: 'The Duke had been so long used to shuffle and cut the cards, that he well knew how to pack them in such a manner as to have the honours dealt to his particular friends'.[16]

Newton himself had personal experience of the Duke's propensity to promise the same preferment to more than one applicant. On 25 April 1756 he received a message from Newcastle House to say that the Duke had made him a prebendary of Westminster. On the evening of the same day an emissary turned up on his doorstep to explain that there had been an unfortunate mistake and that the Duke had thought that *two* prebends were vacant instead of only one. Newcastle must have had a guilty conscience on this occasion, having promised Newton years before to obtain for him some worthwhile church appointment. So, not content with having dispatched a subordinate to make his excuses, he sent for Newton in person the next morning: 'He made the Doctor come and sit by him, he held and pressed his hand all the time he was talking to him, he begged a thousand and a thousand pardons'. He hoped Newton would forgive him for bestowing the sole available prebend on another cleric – and promised to make him ample amends for his disappointment.[17] At least those amends were not slow in arriving: a chaplaincy to the King within a few months, and a prebend of Westminster which had providentially fallen vacant in the spring of the following year. 'The truth is', Newton remarks in his autobiography, 'the Duke was a good-natured man; he had not the courage to say No to any one; he was willing to oblige every one, at the time perhaps seriously intended it, and consequently promised more than he was ever able to perform'.[18]

Other suitors for preferment were less charitable than

Newton when they found their hopes disappointed. And their loud-voiced complaints played no small part in blackening Newcastle's reputation as a vain incompetent who, not content with his own powers of patronage, wanted other people's as well. One of the bitterest diatribes against the Duke was penned by Edmund Pyle to Samuel Kerrich:

> The minister himself [Newcastle] is the Fac Totum in ecclesiastical affairs, & a sweet manager he is, for what with the last Election, & his pitiful passion for the Chancellorship of Cambridge, he has involved himself in promises of church preferments to the greatest degree of perplexity ... He torments the poor Archbishop of Canterbury for every thing that falls in his gift, so that if a thing drops he is forced to give it away the moment he is informed of it, for fear of the Duke of Newcastle. He is as great a plague to the other Bishops, asking even for their small livings. Ely gives him everything (they say, by bargain): Chichester, Peterborough, Durham, Gloucester, Salisbury, &c., are slaves to him in this respect...[19]

Only a handful of bishops were prepared to stand up to Newcastle on the matter of patronage and deny him what he asked. The rest felt obliged, out of either political loyalty or sheer pusillanimity, to yield their rights, while bitterly resenting the necessity of doing so. Bishop Warburton of Gloucester called the Newcastle system an 'ecclesiastical lottery', and so indeed it must have seemed to his contemporaries. A modern historian, Reed Browning, thinks this too simplistic a verdict: 'It was not chance that determined who won the coveted ecclesiastical prizes; it was, rather, good churchmanship yoked to deferential politics'.[20]

* * * * * * * * * *

Many Crown livings were filled by the Lord Chancellor rather than by the Prime Minister. Normally Chancellors performed this duty themselves; though the Duke of Newcastle found the pressure of applicants for places so heavy that he persuaded

18

successive Lord Chancellors to allow *him* to bestow the majority of the livings within their gift. But Newcastle was the exception to the rule. The Chancellors' privilege dated back to a statute of Edward III which gave them the right of presentation to all livings of twenty marks and under which were rated in the King's books.[21] Not unnaturally, as leading members of the government in power, Chancellors adopted the same criteria for bestowing ecclesiastical favours as Prime Ministers, and promoted their own friends and dependants to vacant livings.

Lord Hardwicke, a Chancellor contemporary with Newcastle, made no bones about his practice. In the words of his biographer, he 'thought it his duty to dispose of ecclesiastical preferments in his gift – with a view to increase his own political influence – without any scrupulous regard for the interests of religion and without the slightest respect for scientific or literary merit'.[22] But not all Chancellors were such philistines. A generation or two later Lord Thurlow rewarded a noted translator of Greek tragedies with a canonry of Norwich Cathedral. And to a Yorkshire cleric who had sent him an essay which pleased him, and who he felt might welcome a move, he wrote: 'Sir, – I return many thanks for the Essay you have sent me. Give me leave, in my turn, to inquire after your situation, and how far that or your inclination attaches you to Leeds or Yorkshire'.[23]

The poet George Crabbe was another recipient of Thurlow's favours. As Crabbe's son and biographer tells the story: 'He received an invitation to dine with Lord Thurlow ... Before he left the house his noble host, telling him that, "by G–d, he was as like Parson Adams [Fielding's honest cleric in *Joseph Andrews*] as twelve to a dozen", gave him the small livings of Frome St Quintin, and Evershot, in Dorsetshire'.[24] Thurlow was able to oblige Crabbe on a later occasion in response to an appeal from the widowed Duchess of Rutland, a friend of the poet. Crabbe junior continues:

She gave him a letter to the Lord Chancellor, earnestly request-
ing him to exchange the two small livings Mr Crabbe held in
Dorsetshire for two of superior value in the vale of Belvoir. My
father proceeded to London, but was not, on this occasion,
very courteously received by Lord Thurlow. 'No', he growled;
'by G–d, I will not do this for any man in England'. But he did
it, nevertheless, for a woman in England. The good Duchess,
on arriving in town, waited on him personally, to renew her
request; and he yielded.[25]

If the Newcastle system of doling out Crown livings had
seemed to Bishop Warburton like an 'ecclesiastical lottery'
matters had hardly improved a couple of generations later,
when Sydney Smith, a noted clerical wit and *habitué* of
political salons, was in search of a benefice. He owed his
nomination to Foston-le-Clay, in Yorkshire, to a chance
conversation at a dinner party between the Lord Chancellor
Thomas Erskine, and Smith's friend and patron, Lady
Holland. On that occasion the lady had induced Erskine to
promise the next chancery living that fell vacant to her
nominee; and the Chancellor redeemed his pledge in due
course by presenting Smith to Foston. The irrepressible Sydney
wrote him a fulsome letter of thanks to which, according to
one version, the Chancellor replied thus: 'Don't thank me, Mr
Smith. I gave you the living because Lady Holland insisted on
my doing so; and, if she had desired me to give it to the devil
he must have had it!'[26]

3

Caring for One's Own

'Nepotism in bishops is allowed; – nay, it is expected. A bishop's daughter is supposed to offer one of the fairest steps to promotion which the Church of England affords'. Thus wrote Anthony Trollope, echoing as a fact for an essay in the *Pall Mall Gazette* what he had already foreshadowed in his fictional Barchester chronicles. The essay was one of a series which appeared in the periodical between 20 November 1865 and 25 January 1866 and which were later published as a book, *Clergymen of the Church of England*. It hammered home its message in a concluding sentence: 'It may be doubted whether the bishop has yet breathed beneath an apron who has doubted that his patronage was as much his own as the silver in his breeches-pocket'.[1]

Trollope was not alone in his acknowledgement of a basic feature of nineteenth-century (as of eighteenth-century) episcopal life. Ecclesiastical patronage was a recognized part of the system, to be bestowed as a reward for services rendered, as an insurance policy against possible mischief-making in the future, or simply to gratify one's friends, relatives and hangers-on. As one Irish bishop put it to another when congratulating him on his elevation: 'My Lord, I wish you every joy of your appointment; you will now be able to provide for your large family. You will marry all your sons to the Church, and the Church to your daughters'.[2] A man would buy a living for his son with no more compunction than if he were buying him a

21

commission in the army. Advowsons were pieces of property to be bought and sold on the open market.

Although lone voices were raised from time to time to question the propriety of the Church's managing its affairs in so worldly a way, it was not until 1831, with the appearance of *The Extraordinary Black Book*, that the extent of the problem was brought to the notice of the public at large. It was the anonymous work of a radical journalist, John Wade (1788-1875), and had originally appeared in 1820 as 'The Black Book: Corruption Unmasked', a collection of newspaper articles intended to denounce a whole series of scandals in Church and State. That edition had been concerned mainly with exposing the enormities of the rotten and pocket boroughs represented in the House of Commons; only sixty pages had been devoted to the doings, or rather misdoings, of the Church. The book had attracted steady but not sensational sales and had been reprinted several times. It was not until the appearance of the 1831 edition, however, that it really took off. Fifty thousand copies were sold within a few months.

The sixty pages on the Church had now swelled to 150, filled with fascinating details of a range of abuses. They painted a lurid picture of pluralists amounting to one-third of the clergy, of a three-to-two proportion of non-resident to resident clergy, and of bishops holding deaneries, canonries and ordinary livings in addition to their episcopal sees. Of course there was an element of exaggeration in Wade's charges. He was credulous and prejudiced, but not dishonest. He was prepared to admit errors when they were pointed out to him and to correct them in subsequent editions of his work. In its final form *The Extraordinary Black Book* brought out into the open a state of affairs which had hitherto been largely unrecognized or only imperfectly understood. It was a gadfly guaranteed to prick the Christian conscience. It so stimulated radical propaganda as to become a prime factor in inducing eventual legislative reform.

In his strictures on the abuses of ecclesiastical patronage

Wade devoted much space to the shameless way in which a few individuals of influence managed to share among themselves the most valuable emoluments of the Church – the 'loaves and fishes', as he termed them. Scarcely any preferment was held on its own, he alleged. The sees, cathedral dignities, rectories and vicarages were mostly held with other 'good things'; and the most valuable were monopolized by the relations and connexions of those who had the disposal of them: the Crown, the bishops and the aristocracy. The bishops were frequently themselves also archdeacons and deans, rectors, vicars and even curates, besides holding professorships, clerkships, prebends, precentorships and other offices in their cathedrals. Their sons, sons-in-law, brothers and nephews were eased into the most valuable preferments in the diocese.

As a prime example of the black sheep (or rather black shepherd) of his flock, Wade cited the case of Bishop Sparke of Ely, who reigned from 1812 to 1836 and who owed his promotion to the fact that he had been tutor to the Duke of Rutland. His eldest son, in addition to a prebend of Ely Cathedral,* was also examining chaplain to the Bishop, registrar of the diocese, chief steward of various manors and the happy possessor of a rectory worth £500 a year. His son-in-law received a prebend, three rectories and a vicarage. The Bishop himself enjoyed an annual income (exclusive of patronage) of £27,742.† Another prelate mindful of his family obligations was Archbishop Manners Sutton of Canterbury (1805–28). His seven sons were rewarded by their doting father with no fewer than sixteen rectories, vicarages and chapelries, besides preacherships and

---

* A prebendary's duties were often nominal, so that the office tended to become a sinecure. As Edmund Pyle remarked: 'The life of a prebendary is a pretty easy way of dawdling away one's time; praying, walking, visiting; – & as little study as your heart could wish'.[3]

† So many of his relatives occupied posts in his diocese that it was said that a man would find his way through the Fens by the light of the Sparkes in the stubble.

cathedral dignities. Of his eleven daughters, Wade observes, 'several had the prudence to marry men in holy orders who soon become amply endowed'.[4] The examples can be multiplied *ad infinitum*. Nepotism was indeed far-reaching. It was the glue that bound the whole system together.

Cracks in the glue were beginning to appear, however. In 1861 Bishop Villiers of Durham presented his son-in-law, a cleric rejoicing in the name of Cheese, to the wealthy living of Haughton-le-Skerne, worth £1,300 a year. *Punch* got hold of the story. It printed a cartoon which showed the Bishop pouring over a piece of Stilton a bottle of port labelled '£1,300' and remarking to an obviously impoverished clergyman beside him: 'I am exceedingly sorry, dear brother in the Church, but I haven't a drop for you. I have poured it all into my Cheese'.[5]

The aristocracy were just as bad as the bishops, if not worse. Lord Barrington, soliciting the Duke of Newcastle for a living for his younger brother Shute, made no bones about his pressing need:

> I have but one anxiety in this world: my youngest brother remains still without any provision, which is the more distressful to me because every other brother I have is most happily provided for; and I seem to have singled out for neglect a most amiable and accomplished young man who is loved and esteemed by all who know him; and who has never in his whole life done anything which I have not approved. He has been two years in priest's orders, and will be one of the first king's chaplains that are made. Anything in the church not under £300 would make him and me completely happy.[6]

The happiness of the Barrington brothers was soon complete. Shute was nominated to a well-paid canonry of Christ Church, Oxford, and to other assorted dignities, including a prebend of St Paul's. He ended up as Bishop of Durham. As great a fraternal affection was shown by Lord Chancellor Thurlow. For one of his brothers he obtained successively the parish of

Stanhope, County Durham (the most affluent in England), the Mastership of the Temple, the Deanery of Rochester, the Deanery of St Paul's, the Bishopric of Lincoln and the Bishopric of Durham. No wonder that the diarist William Cole should have observed sardonically that the nobility were 'doing all they can to heap preferment upon preferment upon their relations'.[7]

Sometimes, however, a patron was unable to oblige a friend simply because of the more pressing needs of his own immediate family circle. John Hume, Dean of St Paul's, was quite frank about this when explaining to an earlier Lord Chancellor, Hardwicke, why he was unable to confer a valuable Staffordshire living in his gift on a protégé of Hardwicke's:

> I wish I were a better Patron than I am, & that my power to oblige was equal to my inclinations. In regard to the Living of Sandon, it is one of the very few which the Dean has in his own Gift independent of the Chapter: but for that very reason my Friends and Relations, whom I have promised to serve when I could, would think me very unkind not to make good my promises when confessedly in my power. I have Nephews unprovided for, & one in particular (for whom I desire this Living) ... You are too benevolent to wish me to be unkind to my own.[8]

It was acknowledged by the majority of clergy without influence that the race was almost always to the well-connected: 'I don't presume to find fault with the Bishop of Worcester for preferring his nephew', a curate observed who had been unsuccessful in applying for the same post himself, 'I only wish it were my good fortune to be a bishop's nephew too'.[9]

Marriage connexions came in handy in the case of Laurence Sterne, the author. He had his feet placed firmly on the ecclesiastical ladder by his uncle Jaques, whose own labours on behalf of the Prime Minister, Sir Robert Walpole, had been rewarded with the precentorship of York Minster and the archdeaconry of Cleveland. Jaques Sterne was now in a position to pull strings himself. He used his influence to secure for his nephew first the assistant curacy of a village not far from York and then the incumbency of a living, Sutton-on-the-Forest, within his own archdeaconry.[10] Three years later, in 1741, Laurence was installed as a prebendary of the minster. He had a reputation of being a bit of a rake and of neglecting his parochial duties, but in fact he was a better parish priest than many of his contemporaries. According to the visitation returns made to Archbishop Herring, he devoted three hours every Sunday night in Lent to the instruction of the servants and children of his parishioners in the principles of religion. 'In all the returns I have examined', writes the editor of the volumes in which they appear, 'this is unique and stands alone'.[11]

Another literary figure who was helped on in his career by an uncle was John Skinner, the diarist. In his case the uncle, John Haggard, secured him the living of Camerton, Somerset, not by influence but simply by purchasing the advowson, thereby assuring his nephew of a 'comfortable independence'. Skinner was to hold the living for over thirty years. Earlier in his ministry he had been curate of South Brent (now Brent Knoll), Somerset; and it was to the neighbouring living of East Brent that the celebrated Tractarian controversialist, George Denison, was appointed by his brother Edward in 1845. East Brent was in the diocese of Bath and Wells, and Edward Denison was Bishop of Salisbury. He had already appointed his brother to the living of Broadwindsor in his own diocese; but he was able to give him this second preferment because of the failing health of the Bishop of Bath and Wells, G.H. Law. Edward was awarded temporary charge of the diocese – and made the most of his promotional opportunities.

George Denison was a militant High Churchman; and clerics of that school were not slow to work the system to their own advantage. Arthur Tooth, vicar of St James's, Hatcham, in the

1870s, had been presented to the living by his brother Robert, a gentleman of independent means who had purchased it on Arthur's behalf. Towards the end of his time at Hatcham, Arthur achieved fame through his brief imprisonment for alleged ritualistic offences, and soon after his release resigned the living. This led to a cruel twist of fate. Robert's means were by now less independent. He was declared bankrupt; and the advowson, as one of his assets, had to be sold. It realized £800 – £200 more than Arthur was prepared (or could afford) to offer. So the right of presentation to the living passed into less friendly hands, which soon resold it to the Church Patronage Society, an Evangelical body representing a churchmanship poles apart from that practised by Arthur Tooth. Under the vicar appointed by the Society, a staunch Protestant, the parish's Anglo-Catholic tradition was totally abandoned.

Occasionally a strong-minded or unduly conscientious priest refused to take advantage of his relatives' efforts on his behalf. Such a one was Arthur Stanton, who achieved fame as the saintly and eloquent assistant curate of St Alban's, Holborn, for over fifty years (1861–1913). Stanton's father, a wealthy Gloucestershire manufacturer, had approved of his son's decision to enter the ministry and, in order to secure him a potential clerical berth, had purchased the advowson of the living of Tetbury. Arthur refused to accept the living when it fell vacant, however, as he thought that to do so smacked too much of simony. The advowson was left to him in his father's will, but he declined the bequest.

Scruples of a different kind had been shown a century earlier by the great Samuel Johnson, who, in 1757, was offered a Lincolnshire living of considerable value if he was willing to take orders. The living was in the gift of the father of his friend Bennet Langton, but Johnson declined the offer: 'partly I believe from a conscientious motive', says Boswell, 'being persuaded that his temper and habits rendered him unfit for that assiduous and familiar instruction of the vulgar and ignorant which he held to be an essential duty of a clergyman, and partly because his love of a London life was so strong that he would have thought himself an exile in any other place particularly if residing in the country'.[12] Johnson later told Boswell that he had been frequently offered country preferment if he would consent to take orders, but that he was unwilling to 'leave the improved society of the capital, or consent to exchange the exhilarating joys and splendid decorations of public life for the obscurity, insipidity and uniformity of remote situations'.[13] Talking of a 'respectable clergyman' in Lincolnshire, he once observed: 'This man, Sir, fills up the duties of his life well. I approve of him, but could not imitate him'.[14]

The novels of Jane Austen reflect their author's belief that there was nothing much wrong with the nepotism that was then so prevalent in the Church of England. Many of her own relatives had found themselves installed in comfortable rectories and vicarages up and down the land thanks to the kindness of their kinsmen. Failing a helping hand from a relative, there were often friends around with advowsons in their gift. Jane's brother James, for instance, was presented to a rich living in Dorset by a hunting crony. She would no doubt have agreed with Thomas Gisborne, who, in a work published in 1805, argued that 'the prospect of obtaining, by the aid of his friends and relations, a competent provision in the Church may lawfully be the motive which determines him [the potential parson] to that line in preference to another'.[15]

The career of a 'real-life Jane Austen clergyman' was described in an article under that title appearing in *Theology* for May 1976. The clergyman concerned, William Canning (b.1779), was a cousin of George Canning, the future Prime Minister, and a brother of Lord Stratford de Redcliffe, the future ambassador, so moved in the right circles. In fact he served for a while as his cousin's private secretary before his ordination. Once ordained, however, he had no hesitation in falling back on the old-boy network to further his prospects.* First he secured a curacy at Clewer through the good offices of his former tutor at Eton. Then, a year or so later, he was presented to the rectory of Heslerton, Yorkshire, by Lord Liverpool, the then Prime Minister and of course a Cabinet colleague of Cousin George. His duties at Heslerton left him with plenty of leisure: 'All the evening I have William at my service and he reads aloud to me', his mother remarked of what appears to have been an established routine. But at least he was a resident parson, in contrast to his predecessor, who, as chaplain to Lord Carlisle and his agent, had declined to live on the spot. As for William's curate, he proved to be 'a good kind of elderly man, half farmer, half parson'. Obviously, unlike William, he was no 'gentleman', and so found himself still a curate in his old age. William ended up a canon of Windsor; and one of his nieces married the celebrated Tractarian priest, Butler of Wantage.[16]

Another undoubted 'gentleman' priest, but one who found himself ordained almost by accident, was Archer Clive (1800–78). His father disliked clergymen in general; but included in his mother's dowry had been the advowson of Solihull, Birmingham, which Clive senior was loth to sell. So Archer was duly ordained, to await the next vacancy in the living, meanwhile continuing to live at home and take services at one of the local churches. The sitting incumbent of Solihull died in 1829, so Archer was then able to step into the living. On hearing the news his feelings were mixed:

---

*Canning's letters to his mother reveal a pleasantly relaxed attitude to his duties. After his first Sunday as a parson he wrote: 'I found myself at ease and quite at home. I read the Psalms, passed over the lessons (except that I read the 19th chapter of Acts for 2nd lesson instead of the 20th, but that was nothing) and delivered the Banns with éclat. I was actually beginning to enjoy myself when I arrived at the Litany ... My voice began to falter; the tears chased one another in quick succession'.

> They were certainly not of sorrow, for I had never seen the deceased and I was heartily tired of the objectless life which I led while living at my father's. But assuredly my feelings were not at all those of joy … A sensation of great change, a feeling that I had a home distinct from the paternal one, and also a feeling of the great charge I was to undertake of a large parish among strangers, and I totally inexperienced in every thing like business, whether professional or otherwise.[17]

Clive remained rector of Solihull until 1847. The death of his elder (and bachelor) brother in 1845, followed later in the year by the death of his father, led to his resigning the living and becoming a country squire instead. He sold the advowson to two brothers, one of whom was a neighbouring clergyman, for £6,000.*

* * * * * * * * * *

When, in the second half of the nineteenth century, serious attempts were made to reform the patronage system, one awkward problem arose. The bishops, with their seats in the House of Lords, were among the would-be reformers; yet in some cases, when it came to favouring their families, their own hands were far from clean. During a Lords debate on a Church patronage Bill in 1875 the Duke of Somerset obviously enjoyed himself with a pots-and-kettles reference to cases in which the sons and sons-in-law of bishops had been instituted in a 'very curious manner'. In one instance, when testimonials were in question, the bishop had said, 'The father is a better judge of the qualifications of his son than anyone else', and the testimonials had been cast aside. The Duke left his audience to draw the natural conclusion.[18]

* Much fascinating detail about the Clive family is contained in *Caroline Clive* (1949), based on the family papers of Archer's wife, who had been one of his parishioners before their marriage. Latterly an invalid following a paralytic stroke, she was burned to death in 1873 (*à la* Miss Havisham) from a spark in the library fire which set her clothes alight.

30

A particularly bad offender in this respect was Archbishop Tait of Canterbury, who ruled as Primate from 1868 to 1882. Tait's devotion to his kith and kin, not to mention his chaplains, led him to appoint not a few of them to the livings of which he was patron. His preferential treatment of his nearest and dearest over the heads of devoted but non-related priests in the diocese of Canterbury soon became notorious and excited many disrespectful comments. In the course of a Commons debate on a patronage Bill in 1881 one speaker castigated the Archbishop's frequent acts of nepotism as a 'gross abuse of power'.[19] The newspapers were on the watch for such archiepiscopal lapses, a constant critic being the Anglo-Catholic *Church Times*, which had been hostile to Tait from the start and welcomed any stick with which to beat him. A typical example from the year 1874 read:

> The rectory of St Martin's, Canterbury, has just been conferred upon the Rev. A.B. Strettell. This gentleman has for two-and-twenty years been Consular chaplain at Genoa, and must therefore be peculiarly fitted for the care of two thousand souls in an English city; but then he is a cousin of Mrs Tait. Hardly a week passes that we do not receive complaints of the condition of the Canterbury curates; yet, the moment a living of £400 a year has to be disposed of, one of the enormous cousinhood of the Taits and the Spooners must be fetched from the other side of Europe to snatch the bread out of the mouth of some hard-working clergyman of the diocese that might have reasonably expected it.[20]

Nor were Tait's cronies allowed to escape unscathed. Bishop Jackson of London, the paper reported in 1876,

> has, after a brief period of decent abstention, returned to wallowing in the mire of nepotism. He has conferred the valuable and important benefice of Paddington, one of the very best in his gift, upon that very Rev. Walter Abbott whose promotion as a mere boy, some eleven years ago, on the sole ground of his having married one of Dr Jackson's daughters, caused no little

scandal in the diocese of Lincoln ... On the very same day he collated his brother-in-law, Mr Browell, another clerical obscurity, to the living of Cowfold.*[21]

* * * * * * * * * *

A clergyman was never short of advice on how to conduct himself towards his patron. He might, if austere-minded, heed the counsel given in a handbook on 'the duties of the clerical profession'. This warned him against 'all insincere and dishonest means of conciliating a patron's favour, as by pretending to concur in the peculiarities of his religious opinions, or in his sentiments respecting political measures ... by becoming the companion of his field-sports; or by partaking of the intemperance of his table, and acquiescing in scenes of vice, riot, and profaneness'.[23] But he would be more tempted to follow the advice given to an eighteenth-century cleric by his worldly brother: 'If you expect preferment you must bustle and try to peep after it, as most of the profession do in these days; a friend and application may yet advance you to something better'.[24]

Let the last word remain (as so often) with Sydney Smith. In the course of a letter of apology for missing a party he wrote: 'A clergyman always attends first to those who have any preferment to give away – and, although I am so full of preferment that I can hold no more, the old habit prevails'.[25]

* * * * * * * * * *

---

* The *Church Times* was selective in its strictures, and described as 'very unfair' an attack on the Rev. Stephen Gladstone, a son of the Premier, for his appointment to the £3,000-a-year family living of Hawarden after less than four years in orders: 'It should be remembered that the parish is a large and populous one and that the rector has to provide for four chapelries. Besides, Mr Gladstone has been trained under one of the most hardworking of the London parochial clergy, Canon Gregory' – a *non sequitur* if ever there was one![22]

Nepotism may be said to have reached its ultimate form in the ordained patron who presented himself to his own living. The rapid increase in patron-incumbents was a nineteenth-century development. This was made apparent to the 1878 royal commission on the sale and exchange of ecclesiastical benefices. Those who gave evidence to that commission emphasized the increasing number of clergymen who were buying the advowsons of their own livings. The preferred type of parish was small and rural. The main reason for this was that, away from the mainstream of church life, a country clergyman could enjoy both an assured income and a full measure of independence, unharried by his professional superiors. He could do as much or as little pastoral work as he chose; and, if he preferred to devote his time to literary labours or leisure activities, there was nobody to come and read the riot act to him. Many patron-incumbents no doubt slaved away in the interests of their parishioners; but many did not, preferring to live the lives of country gentlemen* or scholarly recluses. In 1878 the number of livings where the incumbent was also the patron was 753 – one-ninth of the total in private patronage. Some 599 more livings had an incumbent either possessing the same name as the patron or acting as his trustee.

Sometimes a living whose patronage was acquired by a clergyman would be held by successive generations of his family. A typical case was that of the Burrells in Norfolk, who treated the parish of Letheringsett as a family inheritance through four generations between 1705 and 1825. The advowson was bought by Nathaniel Burrell for £120 two months after his institution as rector in 1705. He died intestate in 1738 and the advowson was inherited by his son, also

* In 1842 the incumbent of a rural parish in Lincolnshire was recording in his diary: 'Difficult always to keep up the thought and wish, in society, to be taken for a *clergyman* and nothing else. Apt to desire to be taken also for a *gentleman*'.[26]

Nathaniel (who had been acting as curate to his father since his ordination ten years earlier), as heir-at-law. He presented himself to the living, but survived only three years and was buried beside his father in a family vault the latter had had built beneath the chancel. An inscription above the tomb records that Nathaniel II was 'In Principles Orthodox, In Manner Courteous, In Temper Friendly and in all his Dealings Punctually Just', but then adds a sting in its tail: 'All who knew him respected him, and if any did not it was because they did not really know him'.

At the time of the death of Nathaniel II his son John was only 7 years old. So Nathaniel's widow kept the living warm for him by presenting it in turn first to the rector of the adjoining parish of Holt and then, on the latter's death in 1748, to the husband of her daughter by a previous marriage. By 1758 young John had come of age and been ordained, so was able to present himself to the family living, his obliging half-brother-in-law having stepped down in his favour. He held the living until his death in 1786, when his eldest son, John Burrell II, who had been ordained the previous year, was able to present himself as his successor. This John lasted as rector for thirty-nine years and, like his father and grandfather before him, spent the whole of his life at Letheringsett, except for the few years he was away at university. He appears to have been the best-liked of all the Burrell rectors, being given to generous hospitality. He was also an enthusiastic naturalist: on one occasion he broke off his sermon in order to pounce on a rare insect he had seen creeping up the wall opposite the pulpit. He died in 1825. But neither of his sons was interested in entering the ministry, so his widow sold the advowson to another clergyman – who also presented himself to the living.[27]

An even longer spell as a family inheritance was that enjoyed by the parish of Higham-on-the-Hill, Leicestershire. Its peculiar interest lies in the fact that the most distinguished member of the family concerned was Geoffrey Fisher, who served as Archbishop of Canterbury from 1945 to 1961. The first Fisher to hold the living as patron-incumbent was Geoffrey's great-grandfather John, rector from 1772 to 1832. He was succeeded by his son, also John, who carried on till 1868, when he was succeeded by *his* son, Henry, Geoffrey's father. Henry Fisher reigned from 1868 till 1910, when he retired in favour of his son Legh – who broke the family succession by leaving for another parish after only nine years. Had Geoffrey been an older rather than a younger son, it might have been he rather than Legh who succeeded their father – and his subsequent career, and maybe the history of the Church of England, might have turned out very differently. As it was, four generations of Fishers held the rectory of Higham for almost 150 years.[28] The patronage has now passed to the provost and chapter of Leicester Cathedral.

Family livings could occasionally turn into real goldmines. A case in point was Sutton Coldfield, on the outskirts of Birmingham. The Rev. William Bedford told the royal commission in 1878 that the advowson of the living had been sold by Queen Elizabeth I to a person from whom an ancestor of his had immediately purchased it. In the reign of Charles II the then patron's daughter had married a clergyman, the first of a series of rector-parsons who had gone on ever since. The value of the living was about £1,400 from tithes; and there were about 500 acres of glebe, some of which was providing valuable building land for the benefit of Birmingham commuters (and thus valuable income for its rector). There were three district churches in the parish which would become rectories after the present incumbent's death. His executors would therefore have four advowsons instead of one of which to dispose. No wonder that a subsequent witness before the commission should have commented: 'Church property is so mixed up with rights of property that it is difficult to distinguish between rights of property and questions of conscience'.[29]

To close this chapter on a less commercial note, there is the

35

example of that splendid Anglican eccentric, Sabine Baring-Gould. From 1872 until his death in 1924 (at the age of 89) he was the squire of Lew Trenchard in Devon; from 1881 until his death he was also rector of Lew Trenchard. He inherited the manor and estate from his father Edward; he inherited from his uncle Charles the family living, to which he presented himself after his uncle's death. Charles had held the living for almost fifty years, having been presented to it by *his* father in 1832 when still a deacon. Sabine could of course have come to Lew Trenchard in 1872 to take up the reins as squire; he preferred to labour on as vicar of East Mersea in Essex for a further nine years until the Devon living fell vacant. Charles was no doubt relieved; it would have been embarrassing for him to have had his nephew and successor-designate round the corner in the manor house and sitting opposite him in the church on Sunday. As we shall see in a later chapter, Sabine turned out to be a 'squarson' of the best sort.[30]

4

Souls for Sale

The system of nominating clergymen to incumbencies in the eighteenth and nineteenth centuries was always liable to abuse, sometimes gross abuse. A market in advowsons grew up in which they could be bought and sold like any other piece of property. A critic of the system could talk in the House of Commons without undue exaggeration about the 'shameful auctions' which were constantly taking place and at which 'the cure of souls is knocked down to the highest bidder like a bale of damaged wool'.[1] About the same time, Bishop Ryle of Liverpool, who would like to have abolished all sales of livings, complained about selling souls like flocks of sheep or droves of pigs.[2] And Bishop Thornton of Ballarat, Australia, urged the Nottingham Church Congress as late as 1897: 'Abolish your soul-market. Your system would not be tolerated for a day by the free churchmen of the colonies'.[3]

Certainly, to any radical critic, the private ownership of the right to present a clergyman to a benefice must have seemed like a trade in souls. Patronage had come to be regarded as a property rather than as a trust. Even so unstrident a critic of the system as Bishop Magee of Peterborough could refer to presentations 'effected through the medium of a broker in a back street in London selling benefices across the counter as he might sell so many forfeited pledges'.[4] There were recognized places to which dealers in advowsons could repair, such as Garraway's Coffee-House in London. Hundreds of advowsons might be on offer at any one time; and advertisements in such 'trade journals' as *The General Register of Church Preferments for Exchange* would blatantly extol the recreational facilities and scenic delights of the incumbencies on offer. The going price for an advowson would vary from year to year, depending to some extent on the life-expectancy of the sitting incumbent.

By the late nineteenth century the traffic in advowsons had become widespread, and its professional agents both ingenious and unscrupulous in the manner in which they hawked their wares. It had not always been thus. Sometimes the urge to gain control of livings arose from religious rather than commercial motives. Charles Simeon, the leader of the early-nineteenth-century Evangelical Revival, was concerned primarily to secure continuity of teaching in particular parishes; and such continuity could only be assured if the right to appoint to those parishes lay with like-minded patrons. So he and his friends embarked on a policy of buying up advowsons as opportunities arose. This enabled them, in the words of John Thornton, to present the livings to 'some eminently holy and devoted ministers of Christ'.[5] Thornton, a thriving Russia merchant as well as a philanthropist, put up most of the money for such purchases; and his son Henry, after his death, appointed three trustees, of whom Simeon was one, to administer the livings thus acquired. Simeon himself also bought up advowsons on his own account, justifying his policy in suitably pious terms: 'There is this difference between myself and others: they purchase *incomes* – I purchase *spheres*, wherein the prosperity of the Established Church, and the kingdom of our blessed Lord, may be advanced; and not for a season only, but, if it please God, in perpetuity also'.[6] Simeon could boast of 'my blessed work of purchasing Livings'. His successors, as will be seen, were less scrupulous in their zeal for advancing the Lord's work through the medium of a Church party.

Unscrupulousness of a different kind cropped up from time to time. Sabine Baring-Gould tells the story of the incumbent of a certain living ('whom we will call Mr Baker') who owned the right of presentation and offered it for sale. He put a price on the living which was so high as to deter a would-be purchaser:

> One day the latter received a telegram from Baker's lawyer urging him to come down at once. He did so, and was told that the Rector was very ill ... and was not expected to live. The lawyer accompanied the would-be purchaser to the parsonage, where he was admitted ... to the room of the dying man. He and the lawyer saw the old man in bed so prostrate as to be scarce able to speak. No demur ensued as to price, and the contract of sale was rapidly drawn and signed, and a deposit paid.

The new owner of the advowson had two hours to kill before he could catch a train back to town, so he was invited by Mrs Baker to have dinner before he left:

> This he declined, as, under the circumstances, he did not wish to give trouble in the house. 'Not at all', answered Mrs Baker, 'Mr Baker would be glad of your society'. 'Mr Baker!' 'I forgot to add', said the lady, 'that the crisis is happily past and Mr Baker is risen, dressed and impatient for his dinner'.

Baring-Gould, who tells the anecdote with a straight face ('I heard the story from the rural dean'), adds that the dying rector-patron lived on for twenty years and bought back the advowson for the benefit of his son: 'I was told that the old rogue cleared £2,000 by the transaction'.[7]

A similarly unedifying story concerning the hurried sale of a living is recounted by Benjamin Armstrong, a nineteenth-century Norfolk incumbent, in an entry in the diary he kept over many years. He had gone to Shipdham one day in October 1883 to induct his former curate, George Watt, into the living, which Watt had inherited from his uncle, a certain Mr Bailey. The living had come into Bailey's possession under peculiar circumstances. He had been curate of the parish, and the then rector (who was also the patron) had been on the point of death. As soon as he died the advowson would no longer be saleable. His relations had therefore more or less compelled Bailey to purchase it himself; and his remark that he had no money had been met with the statement that he must deal with that question afterwards. Bailey had borrowed the necessary sum and, in order to pay off the debt, had entertained no company and lived in the plainest way for thirty years afterwards.[8]

The story, as Armstrong recounts it in his diary, had an even more unhappy ending in that the new rector resigned a year later, ostensibly on the ground that he had had 'nothing but worry and annoyance'. Armstrong thinks, however, that there was a deeper reason than that:

> It was said at the time, I recollect, that when Watt's uncle, Mr Bailey, was presented to the living it was when the patron was *in articulo mortis* and unconscious of his own doings. Now Watt, being a conscientious man, has resolved to purge himself from any benefit to be derived from so questionable a transaction. One cannot mention it, but this is, I believe, the true cause of his own resignation.[9]

Poor Watt was never offered (or at least never accepted) another living.

In many English counties the patronage of livings was concentrated in the hands of a few of the most influential families in the county. Such concentrations of power sorely displeased the author of *The Extraordinary Black Book*. 'Spiritual preferment', he wrote, 'is devoted to political objects and to the emolument of powerful families, chiefly the Nobility ... One of the greatest abuses in the disposal of patronage is *monopoly* in a few individuals of influence and connexion, sharing among them the most valuable emoluments of the Church'.[10]

The aristocracy controlled a significant proportion of

parochial appointments through their ownership of advowsons. According to the antiquarian Browne Willis, who published an account of ecclesiastical patronage in the 1720s and 1730s, peers then presented to 1,200 out of 9,800 livings in the Church of England – about 12 per cent of the total. This is exactly the same percentage as that given by a modern Church historian, D.R. Hirschberg, in a 1980 analysis of Church patronage in England for the period 1660–1760.

The most extensive patronage empires were in the hands of the dukes. Norfolk presented to thirty-one livings,* Devonshire to twenty-nine, Beaufort to twenty-seven, Rutland to twenty-four, Newcastle to twenty-two, Somerset to twenty-one and Bedford to twenty. But many lesser peers had their quota of advowsons; and no fewer than forty-nine aristocratic families had at least eight livings each at their disposal.[11] Such patronage could be used by peers for advancing clergymen who might be helpful to them as political allies or pamphleteers, for rewarding their children's tutors, or simply for paying off debts. Above all, however, it enabled them to bestow favours on friends and relatives.

An eighteenth-century Marquess of Salisbury presented his brother-in-law to the family living of Hatfield, for instance; and a younger son of the 5th Duke of Beaufort held five livings in his father's gift in addition to a prebend of Bristol: 'It was stated by those who knew him that he never wrote a sermon; but there is a tradition that he preached twice in the Cathedral in the course of 23 years. On the other hand he had all the skill of his family for driving a coach and four ... and the stables he built at Tormarton were much more imposing than was the rectory'.[12]

An extreme case of cracking the aristocratic whip occurred

---

*Subsequently the number of Norfolk livings fell to seventeen. And in any case, if the reigning duke was a Roman Catholic, his powers of patronage were forfeited to the University of Cambridge.

in the mid-nineteenth century, when the Earl of Abergavenny
compelled Edward Bligh, the younger son of the Earl of
Darnley, to throw up a career in diplomacy and take orders
instead if he persisted in his determination to marry Abergavenny's daughter. His ultimatum ran thus:

> If young Bligh wanted his daughter he could have her – pro-
> vided that he anchored himself to his native country by drop-
> ping the diplomatic service. A surer and holier substitute could
> be provided. His Lordship had no less than twenty-four livings
> in his gift, some of them uncommonly fat ones. Let the young
> man enter the Church, and a suitable living could be guaran-
> teed in a short time. That was the offer, and he could like it or
> leave it.[13]

Bligh may not have liked it, but he accepted the offer as the
price of marrying his beloved Isabel. So he forsook diplomacy
for the ministry and was soon presented by his father-in-law to
the rectory of Rotherfield, Sussex. As he put it approvingly in
an autobiographical memoir, 'he that careth not for his own is
worse than an Infidel'.*[14]

* * * * * * * * * *

In many cases advowsons were owned by clergymen, but some
of these appear to have been no better than their lay counter-
parts. By the end of the nineteenth century a large proportion
of the private patronage of the Church was said to be in
clerical hands. The proposer of a resolution on patronage in
the House of Commons in 1881 suggested that it might be as
high as two-thirds of the whole,[15] though this was probably an

---

* Bligh subsequently moved to Birling in Kent, the parish in which an
Abergavenny family home was situated and which, in partnership with a
group of like-minded friends, he attempted to revitalize in an eccentrically
Low Church direction. He retired into private life at the age of 46, serving as
chairman of the local Bench. He died, thirty-three years later, in 1908 from
injuries received in a tricycling accident.

exaggeration. The proposer, Edward Leatham, painted a grisly picture of the casual way in which advowsons were bought and sold.

At Wilmslow, Cheshire, for instance, the patronage was in the hands of the Trafford family, but for over two centuries each right of presentation in turn had been sold to a third party. The sudden illness of the rector in 1824 had therefore caused great alarm to the owner, because the next presentation had not yet been sold and it was illegal to sell it when the living was vacant or the incumbent *in extremis*:

> A purchaser in Manchester was luckily found; the owner, Mr Trafford, was in the hunting-field, and there executed the sale for £6,000. The Bishop refused to accept the clergyman, because the late rector had been *in articulo mortis*, having died very shortly after the sale was made. There were three actions to decide the question: but the House of Lords, 'in the interests of property', ultimately decided against the Bishop ... The churchwardens speak of 'this monstrous system of buying and selling the welfare of immortal souls'. And they ask, 'What is the purchasing of a living but spiritual domination on the one side and spiritual slavery on the other?'[16]

The case quoted by Leatham was in fact taken from the evidence given by Mr Herford, the Manchester coroner, to the Royal Commission on Patronage. Another case described by Herford and also retailed to the Commons by Leatham concerned Astbury, a nearby parish in East Cheshire ('Now do not let anyone say that Mr Herford selected a corner of the country which in these respects was very much worse than any other part'):

> The living was sold with others by the first Lord Crewe to pay the debts of his son. It is stated that, when the living of Astbury was about to become vacant, one of the ladies of the Crewe family was allowed to stake it in a bet with one of the ladies of the Egerton family, the decision being made to depend upon a race between two caterpillars.[17]

The traffic in advowsons was sufficiently heavy to justify the publication of a number of specialist periodicals. At the time of the Commons debate of 1881 these included *The Church Preferment Gazette*, containing particulars of 110 advowsons and twenty-two next presentations for sale; *The Private Patrons' Gazette*, listing the requirements of between 160 and 170 *bona fide* purchasers; *The Benefice Exchange Register*, with particulars of about 350 benefices for exchange or sale; *The General Register of Church Preferments for Exchange*, with particulars of 306 livings; *The Monthly List of Church Preferments for Sale and Exchange*, offering 453 benefices; and *The List of Church Preferments for Sale*, a less ambitious journal with only 36 livings to hawk. The first three of these periodicals were all published by a certain Mr Stark, who assured the royal commission that he had to do with 'the cream of the Profession'. 'Exchange' was preferred to 'sale' in advertisements as being a 'prettier' word – but, Leatham told the Commons, 'in the lips of the agents the terms are nearly convertible'. Leatham had analysed the various lists and discovered that there were not many duplicate advertisements. He calculated at between 1,400 and 1,500 the aggregate number of livings that were up for either sale or exchange, or both, at any one time – which represented nearly a quarter of the total in private patronage.[18]

The egregious Mr Stark also kept a list of 'black sheep' – patrons or priests notorious for their immorality or disregard of the law – with whom he declined to deal. But he admitted to the royal commission that, though *he* might wash his hands of such undesirable characters, other agents were less scrupulous: 'They are men who are themselves branded with crime and who seem to take quite a fatherly interest in criminals'.

Stark cited as an example of such 'very disreputable' agents a man named Workman ('his real name is Rawlins, but he passes under a dozen different aliases') who was himself in holy orders. Among his victims was a fellow priest whom he

44

had cheated out of £3,000, involved in simony, and caused to lose both living and money. Rawlins was a man of good family and private means, but had been sentenced to a term of penal servitude for altering the figure on a cheque from £8 to £80. He had set up as a clerical agent on coming out of gaol and had bought the advowsons of several livings at auction to give himself a base from which to start.[19] If Rawlins was an extreme case of an undesirable agent, there were others nearly as bad; and the result was to put black sheep after black sheep into the pastures of the Church of England.

There was a nominal safeguard enshrined in the system, in that a bishop could theoretically refuse to institute such bad characters. In practice, however, he could rarely exercise his prerogative without his action being challenged, often successfully, in the courts.

Bishop Magee of Peterborough, giving evidence to the royal commission, cited four cases from his own diocese in which he had been compelled to institute persons who were totally unfit for the parishes concerned. The first was a paralytic incapable of performing his duties. The second was a man who had been a notorious drunkard; 'but his drunkenness and the notoriety of it had occurred beyond the limit of the Church Discipline Act by two years, and I was advised that I could not refuse him institution'. The third case was a man of 75 who, within six months of his appointment, had asked the bishop to give him permanent leave of absence on account of his physical infirmity. The fourth was a man who had been obliged to resign his prison chaplaincy because he dared not face a criminal accusation. It was under the pressure of these four cases that Magee introduced his own Bill in the House of Lords in a bid to reform the patronage system.[20]

A whole string of similar horror stories was brought up when the Convocation of Canterbury debated the matter in February 1872. One case was that of a clergyman 'guilty of atrocious crimes for which he had been turned out from a certain body of Dissenters' who was then presented to a living after he had obtained Anglican orders under false pretences. 'Some laymen waited upon the Bishop, and the Bishop confessed that in this case he was powerless, and shed tears on account of the absolute necessity he was under of admitting this man into the parish'. Other cases raised during the Convocation debate were those of a clergyman who had obtained the signatures of two persons to his testimonials under false pretences; and of an aged clergyman, 'almost a nonagenarian', who was unable to get through the service in which he had to read himself in. Even in the face of such examples the system still had its defenders. One speaker objected that 'some men of seventy are quite as fit for a parish as young springalds of twenty-five', and another that, 'when a man from his property or in some other way has acquired the right to present to a living, it is a very delicate and dangerous matter to interfere with the exercise of that right'.[21] It was to be many years before the situation improved.

* * * * * * * * * *

One particular pivot of the system was the so-called 'resignation bond', under which a priest would be installed in a parish on condition that he resigned after a stated number of years. The object of the exercise was often to keep the living warm until a friend or relative of the patron was able to take it up. A squire, for instance, might have a son still at school whom he would like to see ordained and in possession of the family living. So he would find a priest willing to take it on until his son was ready for it.

Resignation bonds frequently came under fire. As early as 1724 Bishop Gibson of London complained that they were a method of 'enslaving [incumbents] during Life to the Will and Pleasure of Patrons';[22] and, a century and a half later, Archbishop Tait of Canterbury observed that the 'arrangement by which a child in his cradle might be appointed to take charge of a parish when he came of age was one which ought not to be tolerated in the clerical profession'.[23] But the system was defended on a number of grounds. Patrons maintained that the use of such bonds served the dual purpose of providing eventual livings for deserving relatives and a temporary source of income for the bedwarming stopgaps. Moreover, a patron could if he chose insert tough conditional clauses in a bond. He could insist, for instance, on constant residence by the stopgap cleric, an increase in the number of church services held or the provision of a school. Pragmatic and ethical arguments could thus be called into play to justify a practice which, on the surface, was of doubtful morality.

How did those who actually signed a resignation bond view the transaction? Those who could afford to put a curate in charge of their temporary parish welcomed it as an additional source of income. Sydney Smith, the clerical wit, was enabled to pay a visit to Paris after being given the living of Londes-borough, Yorkshire, by the Duke of Devonshire to hold until the Duke's nephew came of age and took orders: 'The living, while it lasts, will make me (accustomed to little) rather a rich man', Smith observed. To the Duke he wrote: 'I have always been poor, and am of course glad to be richer, but I assure you it is a real increase of my pleasure to receive this favour from the hands of one who sustains a great part in life so honour-ably and so well; and this I would not say if I did not think it, for all the wealth the Church could bestow'.[24] Smith drove over to Londesborough two or three times a year to take the service and give his curate a rest. But he naturally drew most of the income from the benefice.

Other clerics were less reluctant to look this kind of gift-horse in the mouth. Jane Austen's brother James, for instance, agonized for a week over an offer from Lord Craven, patron of the living of Hampstead-Marshall, Berkshire, to hold the living until the young man for whom it was intended should be of an age to succeed him. Craven had asked a neighbour to look out for an honest man who would take the living now and give it up at the appointed time. He had been deceived on a past occasion by a priest who had accepted a living conditionally but had then refused to step down. In the present instance the candidate had too much conscience rather than too little. James's daughter Caroline thus summed up the position:

> The value of this [living] was small, but it would have made a very welcome addition to my father's income – yet he hesitated; not from any fear that he should be tempted to retain it dishonestly beyond the appointed time, but solely on account of the *words* which must be used in accepting it. He did not deem the arrangement simoniacal in spirit; but *there* stood the ugly word; and he doubted whether a *promise* to give up, at a certain time, did not go against the *letter* of the declaration which he would have to make [against simony].[25]

In spite of the advice of his friends not to be so scrupulous, James declined the offer.

Another example of extreme scrupulosity was shown by William Cole, the eighteenth-century diarist,* who had been presented to the rectory of Bletchley, Buckinghamshire, by his friend and patron, Browne Willis, on the implied (but unwritten) understanding that Willis's grandson would inherit it when old enough to take orders. When the moment came, however, Willis was dead, and there was no legal obligation on Cole to resign Bletchley. He did so, however, on a point of honour.[26]

The subject of 'caretaker priests' crops up from time to time in the novels of James Austen's sister. In *Persuasion* Charles Hayter accepts the temporary charge of a parish to enable him to marry Henrietta Musgrave. The prospective incumbent was very young indeed, so Charles could have expected a long run

---

* Cole (1714–82) was a noted antiquary and friend of Horace Walpole. For the last twelve years of his life he was the non-resident rector of Burnham, Buckinghamshire.

for his patron's money. And, in *Sense and Sensibility*, John Dashwood assumes that Edward Ferrars is to hold the living of Delaford only till the person to whom Colonel Brandon has really sold the presentation is old enough to take it. Jane Austen's characters as a whole believe in the right of a patron to put family interests first. In *Mansfield Park* Edmund Bertram, whose father had reserved a plum living for him, justifies his good fortune thus: 'I see no reason why a man should make a worse clergyman for knowing that he will have a competence early in life'.

Ailing or elderly priests with a limited life-expectancy were much in demand to keep livings warm for younger men – without any formal undertaking to resign them. In such cases, however, they sometimes defeated the object of the exercise by living longer than expected. Patrick St Clair, when nearly 80, was offered the combined livings of Wickmere, Wolterton and Alby, in Norfolk, by the patron, Horatio Walpole, who wanted to bestow them eventually on his nephew, Horace Hamond. In this case, because of St Clair's advanced age, there was no formal agreement, gentlemanly or otherwise. He lived on and on, however; and, by the time he died at the age of 96, young Hamond had long ago found himself a comfortable benefice elsewhere.[27] And an anonymous cleric cited in a Commons debate complained that his chance of preferment had now vanished utterly: 'When it was supposed that he had a cancer, he was sounded with reference to four livings; but, now that it was known that he had only a tumour, patrons took no notice of him'.[28]

Under a parliamentary measure of 1828, unofficially dubbed the Warming-Pan Act, all resignation bonds were made illegal except in cases where both the presentee and the prospective incumbent were related either by blood or by marriage to the patron. In introducing the Bill in the Commons the Solicitor-General admitted that its intention was to enable the holders of benefices, whether lay or clerical, to provide for their families as they were enabled to do with other species of property: 'It will only render legal that which is now practised in defiance of the law and ... in a most objectionable manner'.[29]

* * * * * * * * * *

The sale of 'next presentations' was always held to be in a different category from the sale of advowsons. The owner of an advowson who was short of money would offer for sale the right to present to the living the next time it fell vacant. He could thus ease his cashflow problem without losing the right, if necessary, to present personally on a future occasion. But, as critics of the practice pointed out, the right to sell a next presentation put temptation in the path of an unscrupulous patron. He could install an old or ailing priest in a benefice as a caretaker, in the hope that the prospect of an early vacancy would attract would-be purchasers and enable him to sell the next presentation for a goodly sum of money. Hence the appearance of advertisements in the trade press concluding in terms like these:

> ... gardens and greenhouses, coach-houses and stables, a com-
> fortable parsonage, and well-kept grounds, with a trout-stream
> and grammar school for the sons, and with the sea not far off
> for the wife and daughters, and good society, and a railway
> station within a mile, and an income of £800 a year [handsome
> by Victorian standards] ... the incumbent [being] 75 years of
> age and ... the population small.[30]

As Archbishop Tait pointed out in the course of a debate in the House of Lords in 1875, if a young man who happened to be the owner of several advowsons was pressed for cash, 'the first thing that might occur to him to extricate himself would be to sell his next presentations at the same time as he sold his hunters'.[31] To sell an advowson would be to dispose of a valuable piece of capital; to sell a next presentation could be compared to forfeiting the annual interest until the living again fell vacant. Defenders of the system claimed that there was no difference in principle between the two, but, in the end, the critics prevailed. Under the Benefices Act of 1898 the sale of next presentations was made illegal.

* * * * * * * * * *

The system of ecclesiastical appointments in the Church of England in the eighteenth and nineteenth centuries was often likened to a game of chance. As William Mason, a canon-residentiary of York Minster, wrote to his friend Bishop Hurd of Worcester in 1791: 'Observe me, my dear Lord, I make no personal request. I only throw a letter, like a lottery ticket, into a wheel, where it may possibly turn up a *small* prize; or from a possibility you may transfer it into some other ecclesiastical wheel, where small prizes may bear a greater proportion to blanks than in your own'.[32] A great many letters had often to be thrown into the wheel before success was achieved. This will become apparent in the next chapter, when we observe two moderately ambitious clerics in their frantic search for prefer-ment. So much depended on knowing the right people: either people of influence in their own right, or middlemen who could whisper a word in season into the ears of the mighty.

The memoirs of the period abound in stories of the ecclesias-tical lottery at work. Laurence Sterne, the author of *Tristram Shandy*, claims that he obtained the living of Stillington through the influence of his wife. The patron, a friend of hers in the South, had promised her that, if she married a clergyman in Yorkshire, he would make her a present of the living when it became vacant. Sterne happened to be rector of the benefice adjoining Stillington, so it was a fortunate coinci-dence (too good, it has been suggested by some critics, to be true) that he should have become attracted to a woman bearing with her such an ideal dowry.[33] But, more often than not, the dice were loaded against you unless you could count on the support of some powerful patron or were content with a modest living.

Sydney Smith, who was ambitious as well as eloquent, found that even *his* irrepressible manner was not a passport to instant affluence. 'You suppose I am to be made a bishop', he wrote to a nephew in June 1827, 'but I will lay you a bet of a sovereign if you please, that I am not made a dignitary of the Church before Christmas 1827. Dignitary means a fellow with rose shovel, petticoat knee and show buckles of ormolu'. Two months later Smith was writing to a friend in similar vein:

> You are to have the command of the Channel fleet and I am to be Bishop of Carlisle – the two events I assure you are of equal probability. If the administration remains in three years, which is not probable, and I am alive and not forgotten, and no great Lord comes across me for his son's tutor – or the brother of his harlot – I may possibly get a stall in some Cathedral, but upon the whole I really think it most probable I shall get nothing.[34]

In the event Smith was being unduly pessimistic. It is true that he won his bet – but only by a month. In January 1828 he was made a prebendary of Bristol Cathedral. He ended up as a canon of St Paul's.

Clergymen had always to beware of counting their chickens before they were properly hatched. A cautionary tale in this connexion is recounted of Lord Chancellor Thurlow in the reign of George III.

A rich living in his gift had fallen vacant which had been promised to a protégé of Queen Charlotte. The curate of the parish asked the Chancellor to beg the rector-designate on his behalf that, on account of his large family, he might be allowed to continue in his curacy. Thurlow put the case for the curate with great cogency, but received the brusque reply: 'I should be much pleased to oblige your Lordship, but unfortunately I have promised it to a friend'. Thurlow at once retorted: 'Sir, I cannot make this gentleman your curate, it is true; but I *can* make him the rector, and by G–d he shall have the living as he cannot have the curacy.' His secretary at once made out a presentation in favour of the curate, who enjoyed the living for many years. What the Queen thought about her candidate's being thus pipped at the post is not recorded, though the author of the anecdote adds: 'We may suppose that her Majesty highly approved of this *equitable decision*'.[35]

Promotion was just as chancy a business two or three generations later, when Josiah Bateman received the totally unexpected offer of the huge parish of Huddersfield, Yorkshire. It came about in this way. The outgoing vicar, who wanted to retire and was patron of the living, was looking for a successor. He sought advice from a friend who was a Fellow of St John's College, Cambridge. A long list of possible candidates was gone through before the don suddenly named Bateman, exclaiming 'He is your man!' 'But who is he?', asked the vicar, 'I never heard of him; and where is he?' 'Why, he has been in India', was the reply; 'he has written a volume of "Sermons preached in India"; and he is now in Wiltshire'. All further argument was stopped with the reiteration of the phrase 'He is your man!' Bateman concludes the story thus:

> Now this Fellow of St John's had never seen me but once. He had been 'best man' at a wedding which I had performed; and we had spent a very happy day together. That was all; and that, in God's over-ruling Providence, placed me in charge of 55,000 people; gave me the patronage of seven incumbencies; made me Rural Dean of thirty churches; and kept me hard at work, through good report and evil report, for fifteen years!*[36]

---

*Bateman was subsequently vicar of Margate, Kent, and, at the request of Archbishop Longley, agreed to take on as curate the celebrated Fr Ignatius (Joseph Leycester Lyne) at an early stage in that cleric's eccentric career. The experiment soon came to grief, as Ignatius still hankered after the Benedictine life which he had temporarily abandoned, and declined to behave as a conventional curate.

A better example of the haphazard nature of clerical appointments in the Victorian Church of England could scarcely be imagined. Souls, if not always for sale, were at least available for casual disposal.

5

Playing the Game

The 'Game of Preferment' needed stamina of high degree. What, for a cleric of ambition, did this really involve? Much wheeling and dealing was needed to secure a plum living. Clear evidence of this comes from two eighteenth-century clerical diaries which, for long lying unread, both saw the light of day in the mid-1960s in a series of edited extracts. The diarists were separated by a couple of generations, but the picture they paint is basically the same.

Thomas Wilson (1703–84), a son of the Bishop of Sodor and Man, lived in London, frequented the Court and fawned on the then Prime Minister, Sir Robert Walpole. William Bagshaw Stevens (1756–1800) was headmaster of Repton School in Derbyshire; the Premier by that time was William Pitt, and Stevens's intermediary with both the Prime Minister and the Lord Chancellor was the banker Thomas Coutts. Wilson was able to importune the great and the good in person; Stevens had necessarily to carry on his campaign by correspondence. Both men eventually had their reward. Wilson's living, when it came, was superior in value and prestige to that of Stevens, who was in any case able to enjoy it for only a year or two prior to his early death.

* * * * * * * * * *

Wilson was the youngest of the four children of the saintly Bishop Thomas Wilson, who reigned over the diocese of Sodor and Man from 1697 to 1755. He was brought up in the Isle of

Man, his mother dying when he was barely 2 years old. For a short time he attended a grammar school in Yorkshire before proceeding to Christ Church, Oxford, where he took his BA in 1724. He was made deacon in 1729 by Bishop Potter of Oxford and priested two years later. After marrying his widowed first cousin Mary he settled in Stoke Newington, on the outskirts of London and near the corridors of both secular and ecclesiastical power. He was therefore on the spot when 'anything dropps', as he put it in his diary. He seems to have lived a fairly indolent – if not downright idle – life while looking for a living, though he was a keen supporter of both the Society for Promoting Christian Knowledge and the Society for the Propagation of the Gospel. (He declined an appointment as SPG chaplain at Savannah, Georgia: the job went to John Wesley instead.) In his ceaseless quest for preferment he was a great contrast to his father, in many ways a survivor from an earlier age, of whom Queen Caroline once remarked: 'Here is a Bishop who does not come for a translation'. Indeed he overdid his importunings to such an extent that he was advised that his interests would be better served if he came to Court less often. His life was certainly one of cushioned ease compared with that of his father, though he appears in the diary as both kind and generous. He was also somewhat of a hypochondriac, but lived to be 81.

The manuscript of the diary is in two volumes, covering the years 1731–37 and 1750. It was among the papers left by John Keble, who had written a life of Bishop Wilson, and is now kept at Keble College, Oxford. Wilson junior was an inspired reporter. His frequent attendance at court and at the *levées* of the Prime Minister and his wife made possible revealing pen portraits of Queen Caroline, the Walpoles and other notables. The diary also of course reveals the diarist himself as a shameless place-seeker; but in this respect he may be considered a typically ambitious Whig clergyman of the period.

And now let him speak for himself. At least he started off with good intentions. On the day of his ordination as priest in

1731 he implores the Almighty 'that I may take no indirect methods to gain Preferment, and when I have any, constantly reside upon it. That I may rather study to be good than great, looking upon that state to be dreadfully dangerous, to be pitied rather than admired'.[1] But the fleshpots were soon beckoning. Only nine months later Wilson can write: 'Our college has a good curacy at Benson, a mighty pretty house and gardens. About £50 per ann. At Caversham a little on this side of Reading we have another at £70. Mr Beaulew the present curate a sickly man. I should be glad of it'.[2] A year later, still unbeneficed, he is seeing Lord Ashburnham 'to put him in mind of his promise to see Auditor Harley to get a Chaplain's Place in the army';[3] and the following month he is writing about a vacant fellowship at Eton College, only to find that it is already promised to the tutor of the son of the Bishop of London.[4] But it is early days, and the real battles for preferment are still to come.

Wilson was for long hankering after a canonry of Christ Church, Oxford, his old college. After learning that one of the canons is very ill he confides to his diary: 'Mem. to endeavour at a Canonry of Christ Church, a Promise of his Place – by Sir John [Phillips], Lord Ashburnham, the Bishop of London'.[5] He is introduced to Lady Walpole ('a sensible shrewd woman'), who promises 'to speak in my favour strongly to Sir Robt.'[6] But alas, there are other suitors in the field: 'Sir Robt. is hardly pressed by Dr Bland to prefer his relations'.[7]

So the diarist seeks pastures new. At dinner with Sir John nine months later he learns that 'he asked my Lady Walpole and her son to beg Sir Robt. the living in Foster Lane [St Vedast's] if Maddox be made a bishop and they promised to use their interest'.[8] All to no avail! In May of the following year Wilson is waiting on Sir Robert at St James's Square: 'Very kindly received and he promised to do anything for me in his power and advised to consult with the Bishop of London what was fit to be asked'.[9] Four days later: 'Went to the

Bishop of London at White Hall who advised my father to
present a Memorial to the Queen begging her Majesty would
give me the promise of a Canonry at Christ Church, or a
Prebend of Canterbury, which shall first become vacant'.[10]
Wilson senior sends off his letter to the Queen, who receives it
'very gratiously'. The trouble was that Wilson junior was low
down in the clerical pecking order and that, for all the honeyed
words of his patrons, his progress up it was painfully slow.
Peers, bishops and suchlike were always speaking up on his
behalf and half-promises elicited that something would be
done; but then it turned out that the sought-after preferment
had already been promised to someone higher up in the queue.
Even Wilson becomes despondent and confides to his diary his
fear that the Queen 'will not be so much a friend as I could
wish'.[11] He cannot afford, however, to risk offending potential
patrons. In November 1735 he turns down an invitation to
preach on behalf of the Society for the Reformation of
Manners: 'I could not think of doing it as having no Preferment may make myself a great many enemies if I speak plain,
and, if I do not, better to decline preaching at all'.[12]

Three days later he is able to report some plain speaking by
his own ecclesiastical superior:

> Waited this morning upon the Bishop of London at White
> Hall. Kindly received. He told me that he had spoken to Sir
> R.W. about my succeeding Mr Finch at Canterbury; that Sir
> Robt. told him the Duke of Newcastle was pressing for Dr
> Burrell, his and the King's Chaplain. That he the Bishop had
> some warm words with the Duke about his pushing for prefer-
> ments and perhaps sometimes for undeserving persons. That as
> matters were now carried 'twas all a scramble, an interest
> thought the least sometimes carried it. That he did not think
> the Queen would forget what had passed between my father
> Her Majesty and himself upon a former occasion and that he
> would not fail putting her in mind of it.[13]

Wilson was still hankering after a Christ Church canonry

and asked Lord Ashburnham to approach the Premier on his behalf: 'He told me his speaking would do harm because he must work by Newcastle, who is against us in this affair'.[14] The Bishop of London, Edmund Gibson, confirmed this: 'He told me that he believed the Duke of Newcastle would push hard for Gregory and perhaps not be denied, which I believe too'.[15] The next day he waited on Walpole, who 'told me that he would do what he could for me, which I take to be a civil ministerial denial'. Which indeed it was, as, only an hour later, Bishop Gibson confirmed that 'the matter is settled and Gregory to have it'.[16]

Abandoning hope of a canonry, Wilson assured Gibson that he would be happy to accept a City living from the Crown. Gibson accordingly asked the Queen for the benefice of St Vedast's, Foster Lane, 'and had a promise of it if Dr Maddox [the sitting incumbent] was made a Bishop'.[17] But alas, there were candidates with superior claims on the powers-that-be: 'I find Dr Thomas, Chaplain at the Factory at Hamburgh, is putting in for St Vedast Foster Lane. God's will be done. I expect nothing but disappointments in the world, especially from the court. No faith in these sort of people'.[18] The diarist's fears were confirmed a few days later, when Gibson told him that St Vedast's had been promised to Thomas by the King in person when he was last at Hanover.

Gibson was soon to fall from favour in political circles, and Wilson was assured by his friend the Master of the Rolls (Sir Joseph Jekyl) that the Bishop of Oxford (John Potter, who had ordained him) 'had now the disposal of Ecclesiastical Preferments'.[19] He wrote at once to Potter regarding the Queen's promise to his father, and also to Lord Ashburnham to recommend him to Newcastle: 'Whether any of these letters be to much purpose I dare not say, only that I ought not to omit any proper opportunity of addressing those Great Men that are supposed to be in my favour'.[20] If Wilson seems a bit of a creep, at least he was an honest creep!

After receiving a 'coole' message from Bishop Potter, Wilson heard from another friend to say that 'he had spoke to Lady Walpole in my favour, who told him that Sir R. said he really thought I was already provided for, which was a ministerial answer indeed and just meant nothing'[21] (and shows that politicians don't alter much over the years!). The Wilsons were great triers, however, and the Prime Minister was not to be let so easily off the hook. On 1 September the diarist receives a letter from his father enclosing missives for the Queen and Walpole and observing to the latter: 'I hope to see even yet the good effects of her Majesty's Promise to my son and your honour's good offices upon that occasion'.[22] Wilson pressed these letters onto the Prime Minister, who at once unloaded them on the Duke of Newcastle, his unofficial Minister for Ecclesiastical Affairs. On 10 September Wilson waited on the Duke, 'who promised to give my father's letter to the Queen, which I saw him do in the Drawing Room. She put it up in her pocket'.[23]

Nothing came of all these stately manoeuvrings, and in October Wilson went off on a new tack, angling for a vacant prebend of Worcester Cathedral. He failed here too, though a possible silver lining was revealed:

> The Queen said that I had a good Remembrancer in the Master of the Rolls. The Bishop [of Durham] replied that her Majesty might be so good as to make me my own remembrancer by having me be one of the King's Chaplains, which she readily agreed to and ordered him to tell the Duke of Grafton so, which he promised to do, and as he can now serve him in his son's election at Coventry he will make the serving me a point with his grace.[24]

This exercise in mutual back-scratching was soon to bear fruit.

Meanwhile there was still the matter of a benefice. On 30 October the Master of the Rolls again spoke to the Queen on Wilson's behalf: 'Her Majesty said that there were 1000 for the

Christ Church canonry but that there would soon be a Living vacant in the City and that I should certainly have it. We shall soon see whether this is serious or no'. The Master then advised Wilson not to go so often to Court. 'I suppose that the Butler had told him that the Chaplains perhaps were jealous of my coming so much there. Alas! Their Leavings would satisfy me'.[25]

There is soon a glimmer of hope from another quarter:

Last Saturday at Court the Bishop of Oxford himself spoke very kindly to me. Told me when ever anything droppt to come to him and he would certainly serve me with the Queen. That there are many schemes in relation to Christ Church and that he was afraid it would be too difficult for me to come in. But that if the Queen mentioned me to him among the rest he would be sure to do me Justice.[26]

But the glimmer was soon quenched when the diarist called on the Bishop at his town house:

He told me that there was no such thing as succeeding to the canonry at Christ Church. That there was no promotion going forwards at present. When there was, if I would learn what was proper to apply for, he would very readily do it. And that the Master of the Rolls might acquaint the Queen that I was well known to his Lordship.

That same day Wilson dined with the Master, who

was pleased to tell me that he had last Wednesday spoke to the Queen in my favour, who promised that I should have the next good living in the King's gift that I should ask for. My Lord Chief Justice was pleased to tell her Majesty that I deserved her notice and that if she was pleased to prefer me it would be agreeable to their Majesty's friends.[27]

On 19 December 1736 the diarist again dined with the Master of the Rolls, who told him that he 'had lately been with the Duke of Newcastle who assured that a Minute should be taken of the Queen's Promise to me'.[28] There was nothing like taking down evidence in writing! In the meantime there was the little matter of the royal chaplaincy to pursue, and the authorities must be kept up to the mark. On 27 January Wilson visited the Bishop of Durham, Edward Chandler,

> who told me that he had been twice at the Duke of Grafton's about my being chaplain to the King. That he wrote him a pretty pointed letter which the Duke answered by saying that there were 3 vacant and that I should have one of them if he had any interest. Complained that the Bishop was too short with him. His Lordship thinks that if I have patience I may expect to have one of the three tho' I very much question it.[29]

The diarist had momentary hopes of acquiring a living held by the Master of Gonville and Caius College, Cambridge, Sir Thomas Gooch, on his appointment as Bishop of Bristol. This leads to some fulminations on the subject of episcopal greed: 'Was with the Master of the Rolls. Says it is a shame that Bishops should keep Cures of Souls *in commendam*. That Pluralists are little better than Robbers, taking that money originally intended and left to those that do the Duty'.[30] Two days later the Archbishop of Canterbury broke the news to Wilson that Gooch would indeed keep the living, which leads the diarist to comment bitterly: ''Tis a shame for the Bishops to keep Cures of Souls *in commendam*. They know their duty calls them strongly to another place and so leave their parish the greatest part of the year to a curate'.[31]

But hope dawned anew on 10 May with the news that Dr Watson, rector of St Stephen's, Walbrook, in the City, was 'very ill'. Wilson at once 'ventured to ask' the ever-obliging Master of the Rolls to 'beg that living of my Lord Chancellor for me, which he was so kind as to promise that he would do accordingly'.[32] But the sitting incumbent was not yet dead, and a week or so later there was an actual offer by the Lord

Chancellor in the pipeline – of a different living, the rectory of St George's, Southwark, worth £120 a year. In spite of all his past frustrations the diarist determines to look this particular gift-horse in the mouth – and is not impressed:

> I went to see St George's parish. Met with Mr Wilson the curate who was very earnest with me to accept of it. There is no house for the minister nor one in the parish fit for him to live in. A large No. of people. Not the easiest managed ... great Irregularities and Marriages without Licences commonly practised by 2 bad clergymen in the parish. Various clergy induced me not to accept of this Living.[33]

He begs to decline the offer, and the Master of the Rolls 'owned that my reasons were good ones and was sure my Lord Chancellor thought them so and seemed pretty sure that I should soon be provided for by his Lordship'.[34] This view was echoed by 'Mr Idle, my Lord Chancellor's Clerk of the Presentations', who was able to report to Wilson that his master had been 'very well pleased with my declining the living of St George's' (so why had he offered it in the first place?), 'and that he did not doubt that I stood very fair for something good in his Lordship's Gift, especially since I had so good a friend in the Master of the Rolls'.[35]

It now seemed that, in the patronage stakes, the Lord Chancellor was likely to prove a better bet than the Queen. Indeed, from the diarist's entry for 4 June, the latter was appearing more and more of a broken reed:

> ...mentioned me to the Queen, who expressed a design of serving me but that it often happened that she was frustrated in her intentions towards her friends by having persons forct upon her by those whose services would not bear a denial and that merit in such cases was out of the question. That for her own part people were deceived as to her interest at Court, that she had never been able to do much for herself or her friends.[36]

At least she *had* helped the sycophantic Wilson in one respect.

On 17 June he was 'sent for by Mr Griffen, clerk to my Lord Chamberlain, acquainting me that I was nominated one of His Majesty's Chaplains in Ordinary'. The following day he went to the office and received his warrant.

Matters regarding the longed-for living were also approaching a happy issue. On 20 September he was told that 'the Master of the Rolls said the kindest things of me, that my Lord Chancellor stood firm for St Stephen's Walbrook'. A couple of months later the great news (for Wilson!) broke: 'A messenger this morning brought me word that Dr Watson [the ailing rector of St Stephen's] died last night. I went to town. Waited upon the Master of the Rolls, who sent immediately to the Lord Chancellor, which gave me good hopes I shall succeed'.[37] Those hopes were not misplaced. The next day Wilson waited on the obliging Mr Idle, 'who mentioned my request to the Lord Chancellor, who told him that I should be Rector of St Stephen's Walbrook and accordingly the papers should be drawn up'.[38] Idle was paid 15 guineas for the 'Fiat for the Great Seal' (then as now lawyers and officials had their whack!), and on 5 December Wilson received his 'Presentation for the Living of St Stephen's Walbrook and St Benet's Shere-hogg and carried it to the Bishop of London. Fees of the Great Seal £18.10.0d'. He was inducted to the rectory on 20 December.

The search for preferment in Wilson's case had lasted almost exactly six years – ever since that December day in 1731 when, following his ordination as priest, he had prayed that 'I may take no indirect methods to gain Preferment'. What exactly he meant by that is anyone's guess. Certainly much of his time during the following six years was spent in seeking preferment by the direct method of toadying to the great and the good – and the influential. He got what he wanted in the end, but only by dint of his constant importuning. And, in his bid to capture a rich City living, he realized that speed was of the essence. The 'messenger' who brought him the news of the ailing rector's death was in all probability a 'spy' stationed in the locality by Wilson for that very purpose. As soon as he got the news he hastened to town to set the necessary procedures in motion. And his expeditiousness paid off with the speedy offer of the vacant living. The race in this case was to the swift. Moreover, success bred success. The diarist crowned his capture of St Stephen's with a much-coveted prebend of Westminster Abbey, to which he was appointed in April 1743. At the same time he was made sub-almoner to the King. Thomas Wilson junior, a man in most respects inferior in talents to his illustrious father, had undoubtedly arrived: at a lowly but still respectable niche in the corridors of ecclesiastical power.

* * * * * * * * *

William Bagshaw Stevens, the subject of the second half of this chapter, was a man of very different stamp from Wilson, though his ambition in life, the acquisition of a rich living, was the same. For a start he came from a non-clerical background, his father being an apothecary/surgeon rather than a bishop. For another he had rather less leisure than Wilson, having a full-time job as a schoolmaster. But, in his untiring search for a benefice, he experienced just as much frustration as his London counterpart.

Stevens was born on 15 March 1756, thirteen years after Wilson had crowned his clerical career with his appointment as a prebendary of Westminster. Stevens went to Roysse's School, Abingdon, the town where his father practised, and thence to Magdalen College, Oxford. He soon established a reputation as a minor poet on the strength of his lyric verses and translations. In 1776, the year of his graduation, he was appointed by the headmaster, Dr Prior, to be first usher at Repton School and two years later assistant master – and also domestic chaplain to a local landowner, Sir Robert Burdett of Foremark. In 1779, on the death of Prior, he succeeded to the headmastership. He was then 23 years old (four years younger than a twentieth-century Headmaster of Repton and future Archbishop of Canterbury, Geoffrey Fisher, on *his* appointment). He was seemingly carving out for himself a successful career as a teacher.

Appearances were deceptive. For one thing Stevens hated teaching. He would not have minded so much if his pupils had all showed brilliant academic promise, but he heartily disliked the task of instructing youths who often seemed to him ignorant country bumpkins. The other great sorrow of his life was his ill-success as a wooer. He was jilted by his first love, a farmer's daughter, and his would-be affair with Fanny Coutts, the daughter of the celebrated banker, came to nothing (she married a marquess four months after Stevens's death), partly owing to his lack of private means. Throughout his headmastership he was chasing the will-o'-the-wisp of a rich living – mainly through the medium of Fanny's father, Thomas Coutts, who had the entrée to Cabinet circles in London. It was not until 1798 that he was offered a living of any sort. Two years later, on 20 May 1800, he died of a stroke, brought on by immoderate laughter at the antics of an Italian and his monkey in the high street at Repton. He was aged 44.

Stevens was an embittered man who lived his life on two separate levels: an outward one of sociability and an inward one of solitude and melancholy. His bitterness comes out in the six volumes of his journal, which runs from March 1792 to a few weeks before his death in 1800. He bequeathed the journal to his only sister Susanna. After her death in 1816 it was inherited by her closest friend, Ann Dalby. Ann's son Robert passed it on to Baroness Angela Burdett-Coutts, the well-known philanthropist, youngest daughter of Sir Francis Burdett, Sir Robert's grandson. The Baroness died in 1906, and the journal was carefully preserved by her heirs until its sale in 1957 to a library in California. In its very different way it paints – through the text of letters sent and received as well as through straightforward entries – as vivid a picture of the eighteenth-century hunt for clerical preferment (and of course much else) as the diary of Thomas Wilson.

The entry for 30 November 1792 is a good foretaste of what is to come. Stevens tells a colleague that he meant to 'make a push' for the vicarage of Melbourne, Derbyshire, and that an application by Sir Robert Burdett to the patron, Mr Sedley, would most probably produce results:

> After Breakfast opened the business to the Bart. He was, he said, very ready to serve me, but Shaw had informed him that the Living was promised to Wat Fletcher – on inquiring of Shaw found that this Promise to Fletcher was a mere Supposition of his own ... Pressed the Bart to write immediately to Mr Sedley. On him he has strong Claims – which he after some faint struggles assented to. But to write a Letter is to Him a work of Great Labour. After it had been composed it must be copied. This was too much for one day.[39]

Melbourne comes to nothing, but the following year fresh hope dawns in the person of a dying incumbent. Stevens wrote about this to his friend Francis Burdett (who was to succeed his grandfather, Sir Robert, as 5th Baronet in 1797):

> I came yesterday to Derby ... and there heard that Mr Hope of this place had been seized with a Paralytic Stroke last Friday and now languishes without hope of Recovery. By his death the Vicarage of St Werburgh in Derby will become vacant. It is ... in the Gift of the [Lord] Chancellor ... If by means of your Interest and Connexions you could obtain it for me (and the obtaining of small Livings from the Chancellor is not I understand a Matter of very great difficulty) it would with my Fellowship [of Magdalen College, Oxford] put me into that state of comfortable Independence which, as you may well suppose, is the first Wish of my Heart.[40]

Burdett protests that his interest is much less than Stevens supposes ('I fear you mistake about the facility with which those seeming trifles are obtained from the Chancellor'), but says that he has persuaded his father-in-law, Thomas Coutts, an old acquaintance of the Chancellor's, to write to him 'and to say everything necessary upon such an occasion'.[41] Coutts agrees, but it soon transpires that his approach to the Lord Chancellor, Lord Loughborough, is premature. He is told that:

> the Living mentioned in Mr Stevens's letter not being yet vacant, I cannot engage myself by any promise with respect to it – The Propriety of adhering in all cases to this Rule must be obvious to You, and when the event happens I shall certainly not forget to place the application for Mr Stevens with those I may then Receive without giving you the trouble of renewing it.

Stevens comments gloomily: 'The Chancellor's is a true Presbyterian Letter. I shall not obtain the Living'.[42]

In any case it was not likely to become speedily vacant since 'Hope, it seems, mends daily – So ends my Chance of St Werburghs'.[43] All is not lost, however. Coutts assures Stevens that:

> from the Chancellor's Letter to him and from his knowledge of him he did not think we should be shoved by on any counter-application of slight weight – that in a corrupt system all things must bow to superior interest, and desired to have immediate notice of Mr Hope's Death that he might renew directly or through some other Channel the application to the Chancellor. Frank speaks highly of the power and influence of his Father-in-law and praises him for his Readiness to use it on all proper occasions. If I do not find in him an EFFICIENT PATRON I shall never find one.[44]

Three months later Stevens again raises the matter with Coutts: 'As You were kind enough to solicit for the little Living at Derby, and as from Mr Hope's amended state of Health that Living may not drop these two years, do you see any impropriety in shifting the application? It must be all one to the Chancellor whether the Living is called A or B or C'. He mentions specifically the living of Norton, Leicestershire, which must 'fall soon', but Coutts replies that he could not ask again till the living was actually vacant.[45] A month later, in reply to an enquiry about the state of play at Norton, Stevens tells his patron that he has 'stationed a Bulletin to be sent off to you the moment the Incumbent should die'. But he warns Coutts of the 'formidable opposition' they were likely to encounter: 'Mr Curson, the Member for Leicestershire, having promised his Endeavours to obtain the Living ... for a Friend of his, and Mr Curson you know is the Son-in-Law of Lord Howe. You will judge therefore, My Dear Sir, of the Probability of Success, or whether it would be more expedient to wait till some more promising Object presents itself'.[46] Coutts takes the point and writes back: 'I am quite of the opinion that it would be foolish *at present* to contend with any Relative of Lord Howe's, and an unsuccessful application would only weaken our Interest with the Chancellor. It will certainly, therefore, be better to look out for something not sought for by so much Power'.[47]

Coutts obviously thought highly of Stevens, and towards the end of 1794 is exhorting him: 'Pray be *quick* on the Lookout. Ministers may die or change and *I* may die – in short there are a thousand good reasons for finding out some good thing to ask for. Be assured I will do my best to get it'.[48] Stevens takes the exhortation to heart and writes to a friend in Leicestershire: 'Keep a very sharp lookout if anything vacant, or likely to be vacant *worth a Gentleman's having*, is to be found in your Country or indeed anywhere else – Spare no pains'.[49] And to Coutts himself he replies: 'The Chancellor's Letter has that explicitness about it which looks friendly and promising. There are not many Things in the county of Derby in his Patronage and hardly any except the living in Derby [i.e., St Werburgh's] worth asking for. What Leicestershire may turn out I shall inquire. If nothing there is likely to drop soon I shall send my inquiries further abroad'.[50]

Meanwhile Coutts has recruited another influential ally, the Duchess of Devonshire, whose Chatsworth estate was in the same county as Repton. He writes to Stevens: 'I got her to write Him [the Chancellor] a Letter which I thought, as you are a Derbyshire Man, might come with the better grace and be useful'. He reports the 'Amiable Dutchess' as having assured him: 'Mr Stevens cannot be too diligent in his Enquiry, and the moment he knows of a Living I will join You with all my heart in attacking the Chancellor and I hope we shall succeed, but it requires Mr Stevens being very alert'. Coutts comments: 'If so fair a Hand cannot stir you to Activity in finding a Vacancy it will be needless for me to try it'.[51] Perhaps he detects a lessening of enthusiasm on the part of Stevens, who now writes to a friend: 'In the Game of Preferment as well as at Drafts much you know depends upon the First Move ... My Patron reminds me that he is mortal and urges me to promptness. I believe that He is more zealous than myself'.[52] But both patron and protégé still have their eyes on the main change, Coutts enquiring of Stevens in February 1795: 'Will that same Mr Hope of Derby resist this terrible Season that has killed so many?'[53]

This letter must have crossed with one from Stevens telling him of a definite vacancy – Wyke-Rissington, Gloucestershire – to which Coutts replies: 'I lost not a minute in writing to the Chancellor ... I am never sanguine about anything, but I can assure you there are few Things more near my heart than Your success or rather mine on this occasion'.[54] Alas, he was too late and had to write to Stevens to break the sad news:

Mr Halket, the Secretary for Presentations, has been here to inform me by desire of the Chancellor that Wyke-Rissington was given away ten days before my application arrived ... It is necessary to success to be very alert and to ask in time – you see on this occasion my asking could be of no use and was Labour lost. I know Mr Halket very well and I shall try to get intelligence from him. Meanwhile I wish Mr Hope would be so obliging as to die and that you will exert yourself for early information on Him or others – for it is plain we must be early to have any chance.[55]

It must have seemed to Stevens by now that it was almost impossible to win. It was no use applying for a vacancy until the sitting incumbent was dead; but, unless you applied immediately after the death, you were liable to be pipped at the post. Stevens felt his failure on this occasion deeply enough to complain to a friend:

Now am I as Melancholy as a Cat. Wyke-Rissington, which You so turn up your nose at, would have satisfied my humble Desires ... I began to grow in love with the very name of the Place and should have thought myself happily sheltered under that said Stow-Wold from the Storms that may arise, but we always value immoderately high the Thing lost ... You may rejoice perhaps at my missing my Shot at This Little Bird which I began to think almost in my hand – but I am very much in the dumps on the occasion. I must now charge my Fowling Piece again and hope to hit more true the next time I fire.[56]

And he assured Coutts: 'We must hope better things another time ... For some time to come I shall be a very Death-Watch among the Ancient Incumbents'.[57] A postscript to this episode appears in the journal a few weeks later: 'Wyke-Rissington it seems was given to the Foster-Brother of the Princess Royal, who had been promised any Living He thought worth asking for'.[58]

Coutts ('What unwearied Kindness this Good Man shows me') remained optimistic. He assured Stevens: 'Twice I have heard of Church Vacancys and twice applied for you, but I hope the Third will be more fortunate and I don't mean to be discouraged by any Repulse. Perseverance may do much – so pray be quick with any Intelligence you can procure'.[59] And, on hearing that Stevens had been appointed to give a lecture on Moral Philosophy once a term at his old Oxford college, he exclaimed: 'I wish Your College would make *me* a Philosopher – for it requires to be one when You have any Favour to solicit from the Great'.[60]

In reply to an enquiry from Coutts as to whether the Chancellor's clergy were 'all immortal' Stevens said that he had just learned that the rectory of Lillingstone Lovell in Buckinghamshire was vacant – but by the next post had to report that his hopes in that quarter had already been extinguished as the living had been offered to another: 'I confess I am greatly disappointed and chagrined. I thought my application would have been in good time. But Sharp's the Word You see. I fear I shall be like the Man sitting by the Pool of Bethesda'.[61]

Meanwhile the ailing incumbent of St Werburgh's, Derby, continued to hover maddeningly between life and death. Although at one point in November 1795 his life was said to be 'not worth three hours purchase', a later bulletin said merely that he was not likely to last through the winter. The possibility of his early demise, however, was sufficient to revive Stevens's hopes of this living, and Coutts continued to pull the strings on his behalf. He told Stevens, for a start, that he had cleared the field of a rival claimant put forward by his friend Lord Moira, who now wrote to say:

> It is true that the Chancellor on a report some time ago of Mr Hope's death had the kindness to destine the Living of St Werburgh for a Friend of mine. That Person however may most conveniently wait. And in truth I cannot assume the merit of showing You upon this occasion how readily I would withdraw myself from a Competition with You because the Living of St Werburgh would not have been very desirably circumstanced for my Friend. I will write to the Chancellor lest He should still suppose Himself under any engagement towards me respecting that Living and I will gladly add my testimony to the merit of the Person whom You have recommended.

Stevens appends to these words in his journal the comment:

72

'What a strong proof is this Letter of Coutts's Friendly Zeal! and how clearly it shows that Chancellors can lie – O Courtiers!'[62]

Three months later he is able to bring Coutts up to date on a previous possibility:

> I have just heard that the Rectory of Norton in Leicestershire about which I once spoke to you became vacant about eight days ago. I had stationed a Letter in that neighbourhood to be sent off to You when the Incumbent should drop. Not having heard from the Person with whom my Letter was lodged, and as it is now a long while since it was left with Him, it may happen that He has forgotten to send it to You. And I rather hope that He has, as I apprehend the Living is pretty sure to be given at the instance of Mr Curson and his Father-in-Law, Lord How, to a Mr Gresley, a Friend of the Former. I am indeed very sorry to be the occasion of so much Trouble to You.[63]

Stevens of course still had his eye on the main chance: 'In respect to Mr Hope, I am informed that ... he has got upon his Legs again and takes his morning airing on Horseback as before his Seizure. Having no particular acquaintance with the Gentleman, in good truth I cannot much blame Him for not choosing to die on purpose to oblige me'.[64] So much for that confident prediction three months earlier that Hope would be unlikely to last out the winter! Indeed, in a recent conversation with Coutts, the Chancellor had actually referred to Hope's having been 'dead and alive again he knew not how often'. In that same conversation the Chancellor had complained to Coutts about the difficulties of his position:

> He said what I believe to be true, that there are but few of the Livings he has in His disposal that may be properly called his own to bestow, so surrounded they are by Government and Parliamentary influence. He mentioned one in Leicestershire, asked for by Lord Ferrers and Lord Stamford, and that he durst not immediately give it to either for fear of offending the

73

other, but that one of them must have it at last or when the other is otherwise satisfied.

In the circumstances it was charitable of Coutts to observe to Stevens: 'To every appearance he spoke with sincerity, and he certainly can have no object in treating Me otherwise, for he owes me no obligation nor can look for any from Me'.[65]

In January 1797 Stevens had news of further possibilities on the horizon. The rector of Blaby, Leicestershire, he told Coutts, was 'in a very decaying condition' and 'at his Extreme Age recovery was hopeless'. And St Giles's, Reading, had become vacant by the sudden death of its vicar. A little further afield the Bishop of Winchester had a glut of preferment fall into his disposal: 'I believe He has now no less than Six Livings to give – but Episcopal Patrons like Chancellors are generally surrounded with a Set of Clients whom They know not how to refuse'.[66] Coutts at once put in a bid for St Giles's and also mentioned to the Chancellor the likely vacancy at Blaby. In March the vicar of St Werburgh's was reported as having 'had a Cruel Recovery and is most perversely well'.[67] In June 1798 the rector of Blaby died, but the living (like St Giles's) had been promised elsewhere. Even Coutts was now becoming despondent: 'I am sorry', he wrote to Stevens, 'that no fruit has yet grown out of the Chancellor's promises, so often repeated, and to say the truth I begin to despair of his being in earnest, though I can see nothing he could propose to himself by deceiving me'.[68]

In August Stevens heard of an 'old sick Incumbent' at Ravenstone, near Ashby-de-la-Zouch. Although, on inspection, he found him 'old, infirm but not in any immediate danger', he 'stationed a Letter there in case the Rector should drop'. Meanwhile, he told Coutts, 'the Derby Vicar I hear grows weaker and weaker, but he seems made of tough durable materials. Winter will try his strength'. He sums up the position thus to his patron:

In all cases I should apprehend where the Incumbent falls from the decay of Old Age or a long lingering illness the Chancellor from the numerous applications poured upon him must have previously made up his mind to whom he will bestow it, and accordingly in such instances we see the Living immediately disposed of. Where the Incumbent dies unexpected there seems to be more chance for the earliest applicant, as the Chancellor if he pleases to favour him need not wait till more powerful Competitors come in. Whether any Circumstances should arise or not in which the Chancellor may find himself disposed and at liberty to gratify My Wishes, my obligations to You, My Dear Sir, can never cease as they do not depend on my Eventual Success.[69]

Two months later the position at Derby was still fluid. The vicar of St Werburgh's, Stevens told Coutts, 'lies in almost a continual stupor, too feeble to move'. Unfortunately, 'it has come to my ears that a Relation of Mr Hope's has said that the Living in question has been promised for these two years to his Son'.[70] This letter crossed with one from Coutts assuring Stevens that the Chancellor had given him reason to suppose that he would succeed Hope but concluding ominously: 'He [the Chancellor] added, "I hope Mr Stevens has no bad opinions", alluding I imagine to Sir Francis Burdett's Politics, with whom he may know you are acquainted and connected'.[71] Stevens hastened to reassure Coutts: 'Lady Burdett I am sure will bear me witness how very much the *reverse* my Sentiments have Uniformly been to that line of Conduct which Sir Francis has thought fit to pursue – and indeed I utterly disclaim the holding or having held any opinions which do not become a Man well affected to the Present Establishment'.[72] So much for any hint of political incorrectness!

Matters at Derby soon came to a head. On 21 November Stevens reported to Coutts that Hope was 'speechless, senseless and motionless – but as he is yet able to swallow and sleep his existence may be protracted somewhat longer than apprehended'.[73] But not much longer! On 7 December Hope died and a letter was at once dispatched to the office of the Lord Chancellor. A week later Stevens heard from Lady Burdett 'to inform me that she had received a Letter from her father [Coutts] stating that he had learned that a Petition had been sent from Derby with the Duke of Devonshire's name at its head, recommending Mr Hope [i.e., the deceased vicar's son and reprobating Me in the strongest terms as a Man of Bad Principles – unworthy of preferment'.[74] The diarist is up in arms and writes at once to Coutts: 'The Extraordinary Malignity of my opponents equally excited my astonishment and indignation ... To secure a wished point they have thought it expedient to remove me out of the way and their daggers have been employed on the occasion without scruple of conscience'.

Stevens maintains that Hope's son is behind the attempt to blacken his name in order to obtain the living for himself: 'A respectable Friend of mine from Derby now with me assures me the Petition, or rather that part of it which so cruelly attaches to me, is unknown in the Town. He has not heard a whisper of it – so carefully has it been confined to Mr Hope's Picked Men whom Himself or Agents could depend upon'. Moreover, thinking of his championship by the 'Amiable Dutchess' of Devonshire a year or two earlier, Stevens adds: 'How his Grace of Devon could be wrought upon even for his Corporation to compliment them with the sanction of his influencing name to injury of a Person whom he could not possibly know anything or nothing at all of is indeed most passing strange. Surely the noble Duke could not be aware of what he was putting his name to'.[75]

Coutts attempts to foil the instigators of 'this Egregious Calumny' by getting Stevens's parishioners to witness to his good character and conduct, and the resultant testimonial is forwarded to the Lord Chancellor. In January 1799, however, Stevens learns from Coutts that the Chancellor has decided *not* to send him to Derby, 'but will give me a Living of equal value in the country'.[76] Fortunately for his peace of mind he hears a few weeks later that the Chancellor is not minded to send Hope junior to Derby either. Coutts writes: 'The presentation of St Werburgh will also go forward in favour of the Reverend Mr Hotham, a Son of the Baron Hotham, who happens to be a particular Friend of mine ... It appears that he [Mr Hope] has not been benefited by his Malignity and very unjust proceeding'.[77]

Stevens is soon grumbling about the 'Living of equal value' which he has now been given. This is Kingsbury, Warwickshire, and even the Lord Chancellor must have felt that it was hardly a fair exchange. Coutts writes:

> Mr Halket called upon me today to ask if I accepted the Living for You. He said it was so small that he almost doubted your accepting it, and he said the Chancellor had expressed some regret to Him that it was not better. He said, however, it was the only one vacant at present, and that he wished to give You something immediately to show that he was sensible You had been most unjustly calumniated.[78]

On 27 February 1799 Stevens rides over to Kingsbury to 'take a peep at my new situation'. The vicarage is 'but an indifferent Habitation', but the parish itself is of 'uncommon size, extending six miles in length'. Such as it is, however, he must make the best of it, and Coutts agrees:

> I took occasion to let his Lordship know what a miserable Living he has given you. He said he was in great hopes that you would find it better ... I am really ashamed after so long a delay and so much said on the subject to find it so miserable a trifle. However, I did not show his Lordship my disgust, believing, if there should be any chance of his giving You another or a better, it will be more easily obtained by Not seeming to be displeased.[79]

Stevens still had his eye on Ravenstone, where he had earlier stationed a Letter in case the Rector should drop'; and in

April he suggests taking up this option, a friend having advise
him of the rector's near-approaching end: 'The peculia
eligibility of the Living, so satisfactory an exchange for Kings
bury, and equivalent for St Werburghs, will, I trust in you
kindness, apologize for mentioning it to you'.[80] Coutts agree
to play ball once more: 'The moment I got your letter', he tell
Stevens, 'I sent it to the Chancellor, concluding my letter in th
words of yours, "that whatever he decided to do I was sur
would be best". In this, I confess, I acted the courtier
knowing the Power to rest entirely with Him, and whether h
did right or wrong his act must be decisive'.

Coutts then has to break a piece of bad news: 'The Duke o
Devonshire told me he understands the Chancellor means t
give Mr Hotham a better Living and as soon as he can do s
He is to give the Derby Living [St Werburgh's] to Mr Hope
Had I known of this, perhaps I should have not have been s
civil – for I confess it hurts me'. However, it seems that th
Duke's behaviour was not as bad as it seemed. It was hi
brother, and not he himself, who had applied for the Derb
living on young Hope's behalf:

> I mentioned the base means that I understood had been made
> use of against You – which I really believe he was ignorant of –
> and certainly had nothing to do with – for a more honourable
> Man cannot be than his Grace, and I am sure he is incapable
> of any mean or base action – but I am vexed to think that Mr
> Hope is likely to succeed at last, and You perhaps to remain
> after all the pains with the miserable Living of Kingsbury ... If
> he [the Chancellor] decides to do what is best or right, He will
> remove You to a better'.[81]

But it was not to be. Whatever the Lord Chancellor's goo
intentions, he failed to exercise them on behalf of poo
Stevens, who, for the short remainder of his life, had to sta
content with 'miserable' Kingsbury; with the neighbourin
living of Seckington (to which he had been presented by Si

Francis Burdett in 1798 and which, like Kingsbury, was served by a curate); and of course with the headmastership of Repton. The quest for clerical preferment in the eighteenth century – for the holy grail of an affluent living – was not one for the faint-hearted or for the easily despondent. The whole system was indeed ripe for reform.

6

The Parson and the Squire

If we are to believe the then Bishop of Peterborough, William Magee, it was the fashion towards the end of the nineteenth century to sneer at the alliance between squire and parson – between, as he put it, the owners of the soil and the clergy of the Church. He made the allegation on 21 April 1874, towards the end of an immensely long speech in the House of Lords in which he proposed the appointment of a select committee to enquire into the laws relating to patronage in the Church of England. He was himself no radical reformer. Among the Aunt Sallies which he set up in order to demolish was the spectre of a Board of Nomination in every diocese to which all appointments would vest. Such a device, he told his fellow peers, would destroy a relationship between squire and parson which he held to be most beneficial, 'serving as it does in a thousand ways to make the clergy a bond of union between the rich and the poor'.[1]

Maybe Magee was viewing the relationship through rose-coloured spectacles. In many cases, admittedly, squire and parson saw eye to eye and worked together for the good of the parish. Sometimes, however, the relationship turned sour for one reason or another – especially if, as often happened, the squire was not the patron of the living and found himself lumbered with a clergyman not to his taste. In such cases Magee's imagined *entente* might turn out to be far from *cordiale* as confrontations arose between the parochial God and the parochial Caesar.

Unless the incumbent was strong-minded, an element of flattery, if not downright toadyism, was bound to enter into the relationship between the two men. There was no doubt who, in the popular mind, was top ecclesiastical dog in a parish. As the eighteenth-century poet William Cowper observed: 'There is still a greater man belonging to the church than either the parson or the clerk himself. The person I mean is the Squire; who, like the King, may be styled Head of the Church in his own parish'.[2] Cowper knew of churches where the congregation might be kept waiting for up to an hour after the official service time in order to avoid starting without the squire, and where the sermon was timed to last as long as the squire's nap. And Sydney Smith thus summed up the inaugural charge given in 1825 by C.J. Blomfield as Bishop of Chester:

> Hunt not, fish not, shoot not,
> Dance not, fiddle not, flute not,
> But before all things it is my particular desire
> That once at least in every week you take
> Your dinner with the Squire.[3]

Some incumbents would go to great pains to avoid causing offence. The non-resident vicar of Waterperry, Oxfordshire, for instance, assured his patron and squire that, in selecting a curate actually to do the work of the parish, he would choose one 'who will pay attention to his duty, and endeavour to make himself agreeable to you ... I hold myself bound in *Honour* to consult *your Comfort*'.[4] But of course there was much to be said for a policy which avoided confrontations. Addison, writing in the *Spectator*, described what could well happen if parson and squire found themselves at loggerheads: The parson is always at the squire, and the squire, to be revenged on the parson, never comes to church. The squire has made all his tenants atheists and tithe-stealers; while the parson instructs them every Sunday in the dignity of his order, and insinuates to them, almost in every sermon, that he is a better man than his patron'.[5]

It is Addison's Sir Roger de Coverley who comes most readily to mind in any consideration of the role of the squire in English history. Sir Roger has been turned into a stereotype of the breed, but of course there is an element of truth behind the caricature. His incumbent had been promoted from the post of domestic chaplain to the squire, being a man of 'plain sense rather than much learning, of a good aspect, a clear voice, a social temper, and if possible, a man that understood a little backgammon'. But it was Sir Roger himself who really ruled the ecclesiastical roost. As 'landlord to the whole congregation' he kept his fellow parishioners in good order and permitted nobody to go to sleep during services except himself.

Another well-known literary 'squire' has been made famous in *Pride and Prejudice*. Mr Collins says it all:

> I have been so fortunate as to be distinguished by the patronage of the Right Honourable Lady Catherine de Bourgh, whose bounty and beneficence has preferred me to the valuable rectory of this parish, where it shall be my earnest endeavour to demean myself with grateful respect towards her Ladyship, and be ever ready to perform those rites and ceremonies which are instituted by the Church of England.

In any context of wills the squire undoubtedly held the stronger hand. Many members of the congregation would be his tenants and therefore very much at his beck and call. Few squires would go to the lengths of the patron of John Keble's parish in Hampshire and actually refuse to employ a labourer who declined to attend the parish church. But they expected a degree of subservience over and above the normal relationship between employer and employed. The parson was on more of a social par with the squire than the average tenant and regarded himself as a gentleman. Even when the squire was also the patron, the parson's possession of the freehold of the parish

ave him a healthy independence of the squire and immunity
rom any threats he might make. A parson could not be
dismissed like a farm labourer. Nor was he prepared in every
ase to turn the other cheek. Horace Walpole tells a good story
bout an eighteenth-century rector of Woodton, Suffolk,
Maurice Suckling, who quarrelled with a country squire.
"Doctor", said the latter, "your gown is your protection". "Is
t so?", replied the parson: "but, by God! it shall not be
ours"; pulled it off, and thrashed him – I was going to say
'*amnably*, but at least *divinely*'.[6] His strong-arm tactics were
choed in Trollope's *Is He Popenjoy?*, where the militant Dean
of Brotherton assaults and half-kills an arrogant peer for
asting aspersions on the Dean's daughter.

Sometimes, however, the secular arm got its way by the use
of force. In 1851 the squire at Revesby, Lincolnshire, James
Banks Stanhope, gave the local clergyman, Andrew Veitch,
otice to quit the living – which, as a 'donative', did not have
he protection of the freehold. Veitch declined to go and
ontinued to conduct services, so he was at last dragged bodily
rom the church by Stanhope's gamekeepers.[7]

Of course the squire was not always the patron of his home
arish. He might find himself having to deal with an incumbent
ess amenable to his wishes than would have been a man of his
wn choice. In mid Lincolnshire in 1851, for instance, the
atronage of as many as 51 livings out of 130 – 40 per cent of
he total – was not in the hands of the local squire. But, even
hen it was, mistakes could occur. In his diary entry for 13
April 1869 Sir Charles Anderson recorded his deep regret at
ver having appointed Richard Lowe as rector of his parish of
Lea. The trouble was largely due to Lowe's churchmanship.
Anderson was both angered and disgusted by his ritual innova-
ions and felt that he 'had done more harm in the parish than
he most Ultra Puritan'.[8] A century earlier, at Shalstone,
Buckinghamshire, Elizabeth Purefoy and her son Henry had
over-credulously' appointed Richard Townsend to the rectory

and had been saddled with him till his eventual death
Townsend's failing was 'ingratitude' to his patrons; and they
took good care to appoint a successor more likely to know his
place. In the event their relationship with the new rector
Wright Hawes, proved so harmonious that his daughter
married Henry Purefoy's heir.[9]

* * * * * * * * * *

It is mainly through letters and diaries that the type of relation
ship, both friendly and unfriendly, that could develop between
parson and squire is revealed.

Patrick St Clair (1659–1755) was Scottish by birth, but spent
the greater part of his long life and ministry in the depths of
the countryside at Felbrigg, Norfolk. There he became the
trusted adviser of Ashe Windham, the local squire. He not
only ran two parishes and farmed his glebe, but acted as
Windham's confidant in all matters connected with the estate
checking the transactions of bailiffs and agents when the squire
was away from home and exercising a general if unofficial
supervision over the domestic economy of Felbrigg. As a
young man he had been tutor to Windham and his brother
and was treated as a dear friend by the whole family. His
surviving letters cover the period 1729–41. By this time St Clair
was a widower with an only daughter and Windham living
apart from his wife, so the two lonely men had a particular
reason to value each other's company. The letters have much
to say about the other squires and parsons of the neighbour
hood and are full of the flavour of the early-eighteenth-century
Norfolk countryside.[10]

A generation or two later gossip about parish affairs was to
fill the diary of another and better-known Norfolk incumbent
James Woodforde (1740–1803). The parish was Weston Longe
ville, where Woodforde spent the last twenty-seven years of his
life. In his case John Custance of Ringland, 'my Squire', was
not the patron of the living, which was in the gift of New

84

College, Oxford; but Woodforde enjoyed the friendliest relations with Custance and his wife, who feature prominently in the later pages of the diary. On 9 September 1778, after mentioning a backgammon session with Mrs Custance, Woodforde adds: 'Mr and Mrs Custance are very agreeable people indeed, and both behaved exceedingly polite and civil to me'.[11]

The Custances had numerous children, and confinements and christenings pop up at regular intervals. Sometimes a confinement has a tragic ending. On 12 November 1780, for instance, 'Neither my Squire nor Lady at Church this morning. As I was returning from Church Mr Press Custance [the eldest son] overtook me and acquainted me that Mr Custance had lost his last [i.e. latest] child this morning – it had been ill some time'.[12] Three days later: 'Went to Church this morning at 11 o'clock and there buried Mr Custance's son Edward – aged 7 weeks and 3 days. The Corpse was brought in a Coach and four attended by two Servant maids in very deep mourning and long black Hoods. Mr Press Custance was the Chief Mourner ... Neither Mr nor Mrs Custance there'.[13]

Another noted eighteenth-century clerical diarist was Benjamin Rogers, rector of Carlton, Bedfordshire, from 1720 to 1771. The main part of his diary covers the period 1727–40 and paints a picture of a practical rather than spiritual life. Rogers was a man of many parts: a tolerant and humanitarian parish priest, but also a scholar, a farmer working his own glebe, a businessman dealing with rent, crops and animals, and a self-made physician ministering to the minor ailments of his parishioners. The living was in the gift of Lord Trevor, a grander figure in the social pecking order than either Windham or Custance, but one who obviously valued the services of his parson and saw that they were properly rewarded. The Trevors wined and dined Rogers and his wife from time to time, and sent them gifts of venison and other benefits: '27 December 1732: My Wife return'd with a Present from my Lord Trevor

of Six Guineas to buy me a Cloth Gown and Cassock'.[14] A
year or so later: 'My Wife and I were at my Lord Trevor's
who was pleased to give her a Lottery Tickett Number
85MO94'[15] (the ticket won a prize of £10). That spring Trevor
gave Rogers 'a Load more of Ash Trees' which he planted in
the churchyard and its neighbourhood; and, towards the end
of August, 'was pleased to let me have his Team to help us in
with our Harvest'. More bounty from the squire arrived in
time for Christmas 1734: a 'Portugal piece value 3 li.[£] 12s.' for
Rogers; a smaller piece (value £1 16s.) for Mrs Rogers; and
for the poor people of the parish, 'two Moidores [approx
£2 70p]'.[16] It is very small beer, this record of visiting and
being visited and of occasional gifts from the rich man's table
(or park). But it adds up to a picture of the harmonious
relationships which could, and very often did, exist between
the parsonage and the big house.

An equally cordial but much warmer relationship was that
which grew up a century later between John Keble and his
squire, Sir William Heathcote, at Hursley, Hampshire. Keble
originally went to Hursley in 1825 as the curate,* but was
appointed rector by Heathcote in 1835 on the retirement of the
previous incumbent. In many ways Hursley was a model
village, ruled by a just and generous squire who also happened
to be a devout churchman. It might be said that he was almost
too devout. He apparently made attendance at church a condition of the tenancy of his houses – and refused to let either
farms or cottages to non-churchmen even if no churchman was
willing to be a tenant. The result, as might have been foreseen,
was that some of his farms could find no takers, as the best

---

* He had been ordained deacon in 1815 by the Bishop of Oxford, William
Jackson, an unattractive-looking prelate of whom Canon Liddon of St Paul's
remarked to G.W.E. Russell (pointing to a portrait of the bishop): 'Is it not
strange, dear friend, to reflect that *that person* should have been chosen, in
the Providential order, to connect Mr Keble with the Apostles?'[17]

farmers in the neighbourhood were Dissenters and were therefore disqualified from farming the Heathcote acres. In spite of
the Dissenting shadow on the horizon, however, both squire
and parson worked happily together for what they saw as the
good of the parish and were constantly looking in on each
other as they went about their duties in the village. Not that
Keble was ever content to rest upon his laurels. He found his
parishioners much less devout than himself, and agonized over
their failings as he endeavoured to put across the principles of
the Oxford Movement to a sleepy rural congregation. But at
least he could count on the support of his squire in everything
he attempted.[18]

* * * * * * * * * *

For a pluralist incumbent it was possible to be on good terms
with one squire and on bad terms with another. Such was the
case with Laurence Sterne. He was lucky to have the backing
of his uncle Jaques, Archdeacon of Cleveland and Precentor of
York Minster, in securing early preferment. It was Jaques
Sterne who persuaded Archbishop Blackburn of York, as
patron of the living, to appoint Laurence to the vicarage of
Sutton-on-the-Forest, a village eight miles north of York. He
was inducted on 20 August 1738, five days after his ordination
to the priesthood.* Sutton was hardly an ideal cure: a huddle
of cottages on either side of the village street and a vicarage in
a dilapidated state. To make matters worse the squire, Philip
Marland, was an active Tory and could hardly be expected to
take kindly to a vicar who was the nephew and protégé of an
ardent Whig. Sterne admitted subsequently in his *Memoirs*: 'I
cannot say that we were upon a very friendly footing'.[19] Quite
apart from politics, the two men were unlike each other in
tastes and temperament.

_____

* The Archbishop was either too busy or too idle to carry out the ordination
himself, so young Sterne was obliged to go to Chester for his priesting.

Matters righted themselves to a certain extent, however, in 1744, when Sterne was appointed to his second living of Stillington, which adjoined Sutton. Here the lord of the manor Stephen Croft, proved to be a man after his own heart, who shared his delight in all his leisure activities – books, painting fiddling and shooting. 'The family of the Crofts', Sterne wrote in his *Memoirs*, 'showed us [he was by now married] every kindness – 'twas most truly agreeable to be within a mile and a half of an amiable family who were ever cordial friends'.[20]

A century or so later another noted author-to-be, Charles Kingsley, was experiencing a less easy relationship with his squire, Sir John Cope, at Eversley, Hampshire. Before his appointment he had made a good impression on the squire being a country-bred man who could talk about hunting or fishing with the air of an expert. Once appointed, however, he realized that the squire's other tastes were very different from his own. Cope took no interest whatever in spiritual matters, never spent a penny on church or parsonage, never visited the new rector, and only occasionally invited him to dinner.[21]

* * * * * * * * * *

The whims of the wealthy knew no bounds. They might even if the fancy seized them, mutilate a church building or even move an entire village to a new site to suit their personal convenience. Edward Heneage in the 1870s hired workmen to pull down the tower of the parish church at Sixhills, Lincolnshire, because he needed the stone to repair walls in his garden and roads in the parish. The work was carried out without a faculty, yet neither the local archdeacon nor anyone else challenged his right to act in such a high-handed way.[22]

A more extreme case had occurred a century earlier at Nuneham Courtenay, Oxfordshire, where the local squire, Earl Harcourt, decided to leave his ancestral home at Stanton Harcourt and build himself a new country seat a mile or so away on a site from where he could view the spires and towers of Oxford. In the ornamental park surrounding the new house there was no place for the old village, so it too had to be moved.

Both church and rectory were involved in the migration. A new house was built for the rector, James Newton, which was both comfortable and elegant. The only snag was that it was a mile and a half from the church. The latter had been demolished and a new church built only a few yards from the old one – a medieval Gothic building said by the Earl (to justify its demolition) to be in a ruinous state and too small to accommodate all the villagers at a sitting. The replacement building may have been an improvement aesthetically, but it was now too far away to suit the convenience of the villagers.

Poor Newton was forced to acquiesce in the squire's plans, though he can hardly have welcomed them. Had he opposed them, however, he would have received no support from the Bishop of Oxford, John Hume, who had formally to approve them but who would have regarded the peer's wishes as absolute. In applying for a faculty to replace the medieval church with a new one Lord Harcourt claimed that such a move 'will be convenient for the Earl and his family ... and not in the least incommodious to the Rector and the Inhabitants of the ... Parish'. Bishop Hume agreed to Harcourt's request as being 'highly reasonable, and conducive to the Benefit of the Patron, Rector and Inhabitants of Newnham'. In a proclamation from the Bishop read out in church on the morning of 1 August 1762 the scheme was described as a 'pious and generous design'.[23] Objectors had only six days in which to prepare a case and only one hour in which to argue it before the Vicar-General. No objections were entered and the scheme went ahead.

The new church was of classical construction, resembling a domed pagan temple more than a place of Christian worship. But its primary purpose was to ornament the landscape rather than advance the cause of true religion. It was approved by

Horace Walpole as a 'principal feature in one of the most beautiful landscapes in the World'. But, quite apart from its distance from the new village, it was handicapped by having neither font nor pews in the chancel. Newton claimed that, with the old church, most villagers had been 'well disposed .. to attend pretty well'. By 1768, however, there were many who 'seldom come to church'. Lord Harcourt had been expected to provide a new set of church bells, but had declined to do so. The parish clerk or his deputy was therefore reduced to advertising the church services by going up and down the village with a hand-bell, 'the like not to be met with in England'.[24]

In the 1770s congregations declined still further. Few candidates came for instruction in the catechism, and there was often no service at all for lack of a proper congregation. To add insult to injury Harcourt had also caused the destruction of the old graveyard and the removal of the gravestones. Many fine monuments to earlier lords of the manor had either been hidden away or piled on top of one another. The former churchyard was now a 'pleasure ground' for the squire – who, according to Newton, 'Mows and rolls it at his Pleasure'.[25] It was aristocratic vandalism on a monumental scale – almost certainly the model for Oliver Goldsmith's famous poem, *The Deserted Village*, composed in 1770. The disruption of an entire community to humour a rich man's whim epitomized, for Goldsmith, the overweening selfishness of the aristocracy.*

The rector had been powerless to intervene effectively, but had muttered mild protests at the changes on a number of occasions. In the pages of his diary his frustration peeps out from time to time. He had to keep in with the squire as a general rule, but he had his pride. So, though he continued to

---

*Lord Harcourt (1714–77), later Ambassador to Paris and Viceroy of Ireland, came to an unpleasant end: he died by accidental drowning in a well. His dog had fallen in, and the Earl, endeavouring to rescue him, lost his balance and fell in himself.

take meals at the 'great House' occasionally, they can hardly have been festive occasions. Thus, on 10 June 1761:

> Self Br[eakfasted] at my Lord Harcourt's & he was much displeas'd at my Milking his Cows too soon and for my talking to Stewart about the Church Yard & for my Saying he had done everything to me except cutting my Throat, which last Expression is palpably False, & told him with a Malevolent Design to injure me & to render him my Enemy; but though I may have him for my Enemy, I trust I shall have God for my Friend.[26]

Newton's surviving diaries cover only a very brief period in his fifty-year ministry at Nuneham Courtenay – 1759–62, when the resettlement scheme was at its height. According to the foreword which Anne Gascoigne, a direct descendant of the 1st Earl Harcourt contributes to the edited version of the diary produced by Gavin Hannah in 1992, Harcourt and Newton were 'close friends and got on very well, despite the occasional tiff'.[27] Maybe, but that is to take an optimistic view of the great local upheaval caused by the resettlement of the village. The rector may have jogged along with the squire smoothly enough on the social level, but the results of the upheaval must have been only too apparent to him as, year after year, congregations declined because of the distance of the new village from the church and his ministry to his parishioners became ever more ineffective. Even so tolerant an incumbent as Newton must sometimes have chaffed at the chains which bound him to his aristocratic patron.

* * * * * * * * * *

A parson who did manage to frustrate his squire's attempt to rehouse him was John Skinner, whose *Journal of a Somerset Rector 1803–1834* presents a vivid picture both of English provincial life and of an embittered priest whose ministry went sour on him. Skinner's squire, James Stephens, was fortunately not able to wield the same aristocratic clout as Earl Harcourt, so did not get his way in the end. The old manor house in which he lived was too close to the rectory for his liking, and he therefore offered Skinner £300 towards building a new house on condition that the existing rectory was made over to him. Skinner refused the offer, and came to regard his home as a Naboth's vineyard coveted by Squire Ahab. He was determined to stick to his rights, even though he ended up by paying three times as much on the repair of the old rectory as it would have cost him to build a new one with Stephens's money.

He was always managing to rub the squire up the wrong way. In November 1806, for instance, he quarrelled with Stephens's gardener, Lowe, whom he accused of attempting to rape one of his servant girls. In revenge Lowe allegedly fired at the rector's dog and, on being accused by Skinner, threatened to have him deprived of his living on the ground that the rector had married him without having a certificate of his banns published in his wife's parish. Skinner was not going to accept this lying down:

> The following day I called upon Mr Stephens; mentioned the insult I had sustained through the firing into my premises; told him I had offered a reward for the discovery of the offender; that it behoved him as much as myself to endeavour to bring him to punishment ... Besides this business of Lowe's I had occasion to notice to Mr Stephens the conduct of his footman, Binden, who got Heal, the washerwoman's daughter, with child.[28]

The squire, however, 'instead of enquiring into the affair, merely said that if he was obliged to attend the private conduct of his servants, he should have enough to do, and never took any further notice of it; indeed he could not well reprove his servants for a conduct which his example had probably taught them to pursue'.[29]

Skinner's dislike of the squire arose in part from the bad

example he set in the parish with regard to churchgoing. An entry for 10 March 1816 records that:

we shall find that the influence of Mr Stephens in times back ... has contributed much to encourage an indifference among the farmers, their servants and dependants of the observance of the Sabbath, which not all my sermons from the pulpit nor conversations in private can prevent. Mr Stephens, when he resided in the parish, never attended his Church nor set an example deserving the imitation of his parishioners. Indeed his freedom of discourse on the subject of religion was calculated to confirm rather than to reform their errors.[30]

Matters had apparently come to a head in 1813, when Stephens had instructed his workmen to fell some trees on Good Friday. On Skinner's having remonstrated with him he replied: 'What's Good Friday to me: d— Good Friday' – and the work had gone ahead. Skinner had then gone direct to the workmen and told them that he thought it very improper to work on that day:

They said they thought so too, but as Mr Stephens had ordered them they did not like to disobey their master. I asked [one of them], if he ordered him to put his little finger into the fire and hold it there, whether he would do it, and, if he would refuse to injure so small a member in the service of his master for a short time only, how could he venture to risk the burning of his whole body for ever? He said it was very true, but as they had undertaken to do the job they must perform it.[31]

Stephens's successor as squire was no better than his predecessor:

Mr Purnell of Woodborough never now makes his appearance at church. He used ... to attend once a fortnight, when the sermon was in the morning, but he gradually has left it off entirely, and very seldom sends his servants thither. How can it be expected that the farmers should be more attentive when they see persons of education and magistrates think so lightly on the subject, and how can the colliers and workmen think there is any harm in spending the Sabbath at the public house, when they are frequently employed on works of labour on that day for the benefit of the coal proprietors contrary to the express commandment of God?[32]

* * * * * * * * * *

Squires could be real tyrants. An example of such a one can be found in the pages of the Victorian clerical diarist, Franci Kilvert. The squire in question, Robert Ashe, was a cousin o Kilvert's mother; he also happened to be in orders himself though he appears to have ceased to exercise his priestly ministry on succeeding his father as squire in 1865. Ashe senio had also been rector of Langley Burrell, the family living; and on his death, his son offered it to Kilvert's father – taking the opportunity of the interregnum to demolish the origina rectory beside Langley House and build a new one some distance away, to ensure a greater seclusion for the Ashes. I was perhaps just as well, considering the friction that was to develop between the two families, that they were to be kep geographically apart.

Robert Ashe was determined to run the parish exactly as hi father had run it. The only difference was that the squire and the rector were no longer the same person. This vital distinc tion seems not to have disturbed Ashe. He continued to regard the parish as 'his' in the same way that it had been his father' – and to behave as if the new rector had no rights of his own Kilvert was able to observe the situation at close quarter when, on leaving Clyro in 1872, he came home to serve as hi father's curate. He soon had a foretaste of village attitude when one of the schoolchildren, on being asked 'Who mad the world?', replied, 'Mr Ashe'.[33] On the surface, though relationships at this stage were reasonably harmonious.

Trouble surfaced, however, in the summer of 1874 an concerned the singing in church. This had been for forty year led by a certain George Jefferies, whose voice was now breaking down and whom the squire wanted to dismiss. The blow fell on 25 October, when he not only sacked poor George but told him, unfeelingly, that his singing made the service 'not only ridiculous but laughed at'.[34] The Kilverts were up in arms on George's behalf – and, in his entry for 28 October, the diarist really let himself go:

> This morning we held a family conclave and indignation meeting about the Church singing. At last we resolved that, as Mr Ashe has practically dismissed George Jefferies from his post as leader of the singing and rendered it impossible for the singing to go on upon the old footing, we must rather than give up singing in the service have a harmonium or some instrument in the Church, whether he likes it or not. We are prepared to give up the living and leave the place should we be obliged to do so rather than submit any longer to this tyranny. I don't think it will come to this. No such luck as to leave Langley. We should all be better and happier elsewhere, more independent, and what is most important of all we should have more self-respect.[35]

The next day a borrowed harmonium was installed in the church. The Kilverts were obviously expecting an angry reaction from the squire ('We expect some violence of language at least'), but in the event all went well on the first Sunday: 'The Squire said nothing for or against, but he came to Church twice ... George Jefferies is as good as gold, no jealousy or spite or resentment at the summary way in which he has been treated and dismissed from his post of chief singer'.[36]

The next challenge was to raise enough money to buy a new harmonium. The squire was asked to head the subscription list, but refused: 'He said that neither he nor any of his household should give a farthing, for he disapproved of any music in a church beside the human voice'. Not only Kilvert was horrified at such a curmudgeonly attitude. On the way home a parishioner, 'dear Sarah Hicks', remarked to the diarist: 'Oh, it's a comfort to know that there's a time coming when no one will be able to reign over us and when we shall be as good as those who are so high and proud over us now'. Kilvert, ever susceptible to a pair of 'beautiful large dark eyes', closed his entry thus: 'Patience, dear Sarah, patience a little while longer. And then...'[37]

Luckily the village as a whole responded to the appeal, and the new harmonium was installed in the church on 21 November. If the squire was hostile, at least his wife and daughter had the grace to admit the next day after morning service that they liked the instrument. But there was something else in church that morning to which Squire Ashe took exception: the first fire of the winter. 'As soon as he saw or smelt the fire in the stove he turned round and went hastily out again'.[38] He was obviously a fresh-air fiend and disapproved of namby-pamby attitudes to cold weather. Only a few days earlier he had caused trouble at the school by ordering the teacher always to keep all three windows and the door of the school-room open during schooltime ('except in very cold weather, when one window might be shut'). Kilvert concludes his diary entry for that day:

> He said in a fierce determined way, 'This is my school and I will have my word attended to. If you don't do as I tell you, Miss Bland, instead of being your friend I'll be your enemy'. What a speech for an elderly clergyman. It is almost incredible. And there are the poor little children crying with the cold. Cruel. Barbarous. And of course the parents are indignant and the numbers of the children falling off.[39]

The squire's attitude to heating in church softened over the years. But his dismissal of the choir-leader and his peremptory attitude towards the schoolmistress are symptomatic of the unfettered power possessed by a country squire in Victorian England.

* * * * * * * * * *

96

The most detailed account of a relationship between a parson and his squire is that described by Owen Chadwick in his fascinating *A Victorian Miniature*. The period is the middle part of the nineteenth century and the area rural Norfolk. The relationship can be studied in detail because the diaries of the parson and squire in question, William Andrew and Sir John Boileau, have both survived.

It was in 1835 that Andrew became vicar of the tiny parish of Ketteringham – three years before Boileau, the new owner of Ketteringham Hall, took up residence there. Both were men of principle, and their principles not infrequently clashed. Sir John was a good landlord and a devout Christian. But he was no puritan, and resented being rebuked by Andrew for alleged sabbath-breaking and for allowing dancing at the Hall. Like Robert Ashe at Langley Burrell, he was high-handed in his dealings with the vicar, whom he failed to consult when he decided to alter and improve the church. He also, like Ashe, regarded the schoolmistress, Sarah Cooper, as if she was one of his personal servants. This caused grave problems for Sarah. She admired the vicar and tried to conduct her school in a manner which he would approve. But she was dependent on the squire for her salary and could not afford to offend him if he wanted things handled differently. On one occasion, when she was summoned by the squire to a New Year ball of which the vicar disapproved, she could only excuse her absence by feigning illness. There was yet another source of disagreement between the two men. The squire thought that the church should be reserved for people resident in the parish: the vicar felt that it should be open to all who wished to attend services there.

In exercising his presumed right to treat the church as his own private property Sir John at last overstepped himself. His wife was very ill and expected to die. He wished her to be buried in the chancel vault, which was overcrowded as it was. So he simply had the other coffins removed and reburied in the churchyard without benefit of faculty. Andrew was well aware of the illegality of the action, but kept smugly silent. Nemesis soon followed when a relative of one of the uprooted dead objected publicly; eventually, after an enquiry, the squire was forced to eat humble pie and return the coffins to the chancel vault. He was not amused, and felt that the vicar should have put him wise before the event.

There was a Jekyll-and-Hyde element in the relationship between the two men. The vicar would visit the squire when he was ill and talk easily with him on spiritual matters. But then a quarrel would take place, for example over the alterations being made to the church without Andrew's consent, which would lead to the following sort of remark: 'I cannot see', said Sir John, 'that your conduct is at all more important than mine. I am as answerable for the souls of my parish as you are. There is not the least difference in our situations except that I cannot perform the services of the church'.[40] At least in his sermons the vicar could have a go at the squire without fear of interruption. But his attacks, however veiled, did not go unremarked by the rest of the congregation: 'O sir', a servant of the squire's remarked to Andrew on one occasion, 'how hard you do strike Sir John in your sermons! I really do not know scarcely how to sit sometimes in my seat'.[41] The vicar might be preaching against sabbath-breaking in general terms, but the villagers would interpret his strictures as being directed personally against the squire.

Nevertheless, in spite of their differences of opinion, the squire, as he grew older (and especially after the death of his wife), became reconciled to Andrew. His unmarried daughters found themselves drawn towards the vicar's intrinsic goodness, and he himself came to accept Andrew's spiritual direction. As Chadwick comments: 'He had succumbed, in some part, to the courage, the integrity, and the perseverance of the vicar ... but still more to the insistent cry of the human soul, in the end, for the consolation of the spirit'.[42]

* * * * * * * * * *

It helped of course if the squire *was* the parson, as sometimes happened. A fine example of a 'squarson' was Sabine Baring-Gould, author of 'Onward, Christian Soldiers' and of much else. His forty-three years as rector and fifty-two as squire of Lew Trenchard in Devon had been preceded by a less happy period as perpetual curate of Dalton, an East Riding hamlet known as 'Dalton i't Muck', to which he had been appointed by Archbishop Thomson of York* shortly after his marriage to a mill-hand's daughter. The squire, or rather lady of the manor, with whom he had to deal in this muddy backwater was the Viscountess Downe; besides being the widow of a peer, she was also the daughter of a Bishop of Bath and Wells. She was a tartar in church matters, selecting the hymns personally and insisting on short sermons: transgressing the allotted time was likely to be punished by a temporary cutting off of the supply of wine and fruit from the manor to the parsonage. Eventually Baring-Gould, thanks to an offer from Mr Gladstone, was able to move to the Crown living of East Mersea, though it is doubtful if he found the Essex sea-flats much more congenial than the Yorkshire mud. But he soldiered on there until the death of his uncle, Charles Baring-Gould, enabled him to appoint himself to the family living. For nine years previously, ever since his father's death in 1872, he had been the absentee squire of Lew Trenchard.

As a 'squarson' he was a kindly despot, of the type who recognized duties as well as rights. He was concerned as squire for the material well-being of his parishioners and as parson

---

* Of whom Baring-Gould had a low opinion! He says in his *Further Reminiscences*: 'He [Thomson] possessed an autocratic and masterful temper, such as was naturally bred in a man rapidly advanced from a breeches-maker's shop in a small provincial town to positions of great authority'.[43] But then he may have been offended by Thomson's taking no notice of him – he even suggests that the Archbishop had placed him on a private 'black-list'.

for the good of their souls. The villagers were expected to touch their caps or curtsey to the squire, but they knew that, in times of sickness or misfortune, they could go to the big house for comfort or assistance. He could never say no to anybody who came to him for help. It was paternalism, but paternalism at its best. He was always considerate in his dealings with his people. When he went in his dog-cart to visit his workmen he had bells put on the pony to warn the men that he was coming. Nor, when he plugged his ears with cotton-wool if a particular parishioner whose singing he abominated was in the choir, would he have dreamed of letting them know of his action.

As a priest he had two objects in view at Lew Trenchard: to teach the people to love God and to be true to the Catholic Church. He told one of his churchwardens towards the end of his life: 'I feel deeply how little I have effected through my own shortcomings. But I trust that at the Last Day, when I stand in self-conscious humiliation before the throne of God, you and some others here will be able to speak a word for me'.[44]

7

Safety in Numbers

Patronage was not always exercised by a single individual. Sometimes, as in the case of a dean and chapter, it was a corporate perquisite belonging to a body of men who needed to come to a majority decision. Among these corporate bodies were the universities of Oxford and Cambridge and their constituent colleges. The colleges occupied a special position, in that the numerous livings at their disposal were almost invariably bestowed on their own fellows. Indeed the exchange in due course of fellowships for livings was an essential part of the Oxbridge college system. It was a classic case of jobs for the boys.

So long as college fellows had to be in orders, the colleges were bound by custom to offer each living in their gift which became vacant to the senior fellow – who might or might not be the best man for the job. Sometimes the fellows might be considered long past their sell-by date, so that, as the report of the mid-nineteenth-century Oxford University Commission sardonically observed, by the time they were finally offered a living they were 'fit neither for the post they have coveted, nor for any other'.[1] Lord Egmont, a leading opponent of college patronage in the 1730s, thought that the seniority rule was a great discouragement to study, 'for a learned man shall not have the preference over a blockhead, because it is not his turn'.[2]

Most college fellows would hope to spend the greater part of their career in a living – which, besides giving them an independent and better-paid sphere of work, also enabled them to marry, a privilege not permitted to fellows until 1882. The snag in the system was that it tended to discourage original research, or indeed exertion of any sort, on the part of unmarried college dons. Why waste time, they argued, on lines of enquiry which could be fruitful with a well-stocked college library to hand but which would be much harder to pursue once they had been appointed to an isolated rural rectory? As Robert Danny, a promising scientist, complained from his Yorkshire benefice to a former pupil: 'Look upon me as a Lover of Learning destitute of some of the principal means of Improvement, and consequently rusting in a Desert'.[3]

It suited the colleges to acquire livings, so that, as vacancies arose, they could be filled with a constant flow of fellows. The improvement of the livings thus acquired provided a useful channel for the investment of surplus funds, the livings being looked upon as extensions of the college. The steady rise in the number of college livings was opposed by those who argued that such an increase represented a dangerous rise in clerical influence and, in the words of one critic, 'would render the clergy independent of the laity'.[4] The argument was a weak one, in that, at many of the colleges, few of the fellows were promoted to a living before they had served for many years as a fellow. As an Oxford vice-chancellor commented, 'there is no great danger of our becoming too powerfull with relation to advowsons, supposing no Restraint at all was laid upon us in this point'.[5]

An anti-clerical campaign in the 1730s was politically motivated. It was due largely to the weakening position of the Prime Minister, Robert Walpole, in relation to his anti-clerical opponents. The attack in Parliament took the form of a Bill designed in part to place severe restrictions on the number of advowsons which colleges could purchase. The universities defended themselves vigorously against their critics. An Oxford pamphlet pointed out that several colleges possessed no livings at all, and others only two or three of moderate value: 'None of them have so many, and of such Value, that it can possibly be any reasonable Invitation to the Fellows of those Colleges to rest their Hopes of Preferment there; or to make them indolent or less careful to recommend themselves to the Patronage of others'.[6] When the Bill came to be debated in Parliament, vigorous lobbying succeeded in watering down its restrictive clauses.* An attempt to freeze the number of advowsons held by the colleges at their existing level was defeated in favour of a clause permitting them to purchase advowsons up to a maximum of half their fellowships. Even this limited restraint lasted a bare seventy years. It was repealed in 1805 by the University Advowsons Act, on the ground that such an artificial restriction made the succession of fellows to livings far too slow, and that its abolition would lead to a better supply of 'fit and competent Parochial Ministers'.[7]

What was the extent of university patronage? Oxford and its colleges in the early eighteenth century possessed about 290 livings and Cambridge (with 130 fewer fellows) about 250. In spite of the modest curbs of the Act the colleges in both universities had managed, by the end of the century, to increase the number of livings in their gift by about 20 per cent. Following the passing of the University Advowsons Act in 1805 there was a further modest increase.

Although each college living as it fell vacant was offered first to the senior fellow, he would sometimes refuse it. The memoirs and letters of the period often include references to such self-abnegation on the part of senior dons. Thus Richard Radcliffe, writing to his friend John James senior in 1778, observes that he has just accepted the benefice of Holwell, Somerset, in the gift of Queen's College, Oxford, on a senior

---

* Walpole himself did a great deal behind the scenes to counter the effect of the radical Whigs, and to whip up support for exceptions and exemptions designed to emasculate the Bill.

don's having given up his claim to it. And he tells James that, when the living had last fallen vacant in 1775, 'the preferment was so little known, or thought so indifferent at that time, that six or seven of the Seniors refused it' before it was accepted by his predecessor, Thomas Hobson, who had improved its revenues and put all its buildings into excellent order. As a result Radcliffe felt it well worth accepting: 'Holwell, in point of income, is inferior (I believe) to many of our College preferments; but there were some circumstances that seemed to recommend it to me – only one church – never a Squire, nay, nothing above the degree of a petty constable; not to mention the house and premises'.[8]*

Another and better-known cleric able to avail himself of a living through a senior don's waiving his claim to it was the diarist James Woodforde. He was a Fellow of New College, Oxford; and the living concerned was Weston Longeville, Norfolk, which fell vacant in 1774. The most senior fellow declined the living, so, Woodforde confides to his diary, 'I therefore immediately being the next Senior in Orders canvassed the Senior Common Room, and then went ... into the Junior Common Room & canvassed that'. At New College it was not the custom automatically to award a living to the second senior don if the most senior declined it, so Woodforde found himself facing a rival candidate – and a contested election: 'Many learned and warm arguments started and disputed, and after 2 hours debate the House divided and it was put to the Vote, when there appeared for me 21 votes, for Mr Hooke 15 only, on which I was declared and presented with the Presentation of the Rectory'. (Woodforde had

---

* The parish also intrigued Radcliffe as lying between Sherborne and Blandford, and yet being a part of Somerset, 'and in every respect belongs to that county, though detached from it by a space of four miles and surrounded on every side by Dorsetshire'. Radcliffe had been a fellow of Queen's since 1762; he was to remain rector of Holwell till his death in 1793.

104

prudently voted for himself, though Hooke abstained.) The diarist's supporters deserved to be rewarded, so, he concludes, 'I treated the Senr. Com. Room with Wine and Fruit in the afternoon and in the evening with Arrac Punch and Wine. I treated the Junr. Com. Room with one dozen of Wine afternoon and in the evening with Arrac Punch and Wine. I gave the Chaplains half a dozen of Wine, the clerks 2 bottles and the Steward one bottle'.[9]

Woodforde took his time in setting about his new duties, not taking up residence at Weston Longeville till 1776. But he spent the last twenty-seven years of his life there.

At Merton, another Oxford college, Mandell Creighton, the future Bishop of London, was spared the hazard of a contested election when, exactly a century later, the two dons immediately senior to him both refused the living of Embleton, Northumberland. In Creighton's case the only delay in acceptance was due to his inability to make up his mind. He was a born scholar and an inspired teacher; and a letter signed by thirty-six of the senior undergraduates implored him to stay: 'We think that your departure would cause us an irreparable loss both in the lecture-room and in the management of the College'. But Creighton's older friends urged him to take the living and in the end he did so, in the belief that a country benefice would give him more freedom to complete his long-projected history of the Papacy than the manifold activities required of him by his college duties.*[10]

Some Oxbridge colleges bought up advowsons as a matter of policy in order to provide for senior fellows frustrated at their inability to escape the academic grind. But, at £1,000 or more for a well-endowed living, this was an option only possible for

---

*His friend Mark Pattison was highly critical of his decision. 'What are you going into the country for?' 'To study history'; 'You can't study history without a library, and you can't get an adequate historical library unless you spend at least £1000 a year on books'.

the more affluent colleges. In a class of its own was Chris
Church, Oxford, whose chapel doubled as cathedral for the
diocese and which therefore possessed more livings than any
other Oxford college – fifteen in the diocese alone, compared
with the thirty-nine belonging in 1777 to the other thirteen
advowson-owning colleges combined.[11]

Sometimes a college miscalculated the attractions of a
benefice it was seeking to acquire. Thus, in 1824, Oriel
Oxford, purchased the living of Twerton, an agricultural
suburb of Bath pleasantly situated on the banks of the Avon,
under the impression, first, that it was inhabited by the 'right
sort' of people and, secondly, that its present incumbent would
shortly die. Unfortunately for the college, the ailing rector
declined to bow out before the living had completely changed
its character through the industrial growth brought about by
the new Great Western Railway. It no longer attracted the
'right sort' of people, and therefore proved much less of a lure
to ageing dons looking for a quiet berth on the edge of the
country.[12]

Sometimes, again, a college got into difficulties through
sheer mischance. In 1755 the vicar of Hitchin, Hertfordshire, a
living in the gift of Trinity, Cambridge, was promoted to the
bishopric of Sodor and Man. Normally, when a living fell
vacant in this way, its patronage passed to the Crown for that
turn; so the Duke of Newcastle, on the Crown's behalf, offered
the living to the curate of Hitchin, whose claims were
supported by the town's parishioners. This annoyed the Master
and fellows of Trinity because, as they pointed out to
Newcastle, the curate was a graduate of Oxford, not
Cambridge, and they had 'very few livings in their gift for
which a Fellow would quit his Fellowship'. The strength of
their case lay in a point of law. The see of Sodor and Man was
different from other English bishoprics, in that the sovereignty
of the Isle of Man was at that time vested in the House of
Athol, not the House of Hanover; it could therefore be argued

106

that the patronage of Hitchin had not passed automatically to
the Crown for that turn but was still vested in the college. The
fellows pressed their case with vigour. Newcastle, on the advice
of the Crown lawyers, was at first inclined to do battle; he then
weakened a little and suggested putting the matter to arbitration; in the end, mindful of his position as Chancellor of
Cambridge University and not wishing to be in Trinity's black
books, he gave way gracefully and allowed its nominee, a
fellow of the college, to take possession of the living.[13]

* * * * * * * * * *

A very different form of corporate patronage was when it lay
either with the parishioners of a benefice or, more commonly,
with a body of trustees acting on their behalf. Only a small
number of livings enjoyed this type of patronage; but, when
one fell vacant, the resultant election of a new incumbent
sometimes produced much sound and fury.

It might have been supposed that such a seemingly
democratic way of appointing an incumbent would have
attracted widespread support. But there were obvious dangers.
As Thomas Gisborne pointed out in a book published in 1805,
private patronage was intended to remedy:

> the many disorders and evils which would be likely to arise in
> this country were the choice left to be determined in each
> parish by the suffrages of the inhabitants ... The parish would
> be assailed with every art practised in a venal borough ... the
> flame of contention would break forth ... the benefice would be
> the prize, not of piety and merit, but of private tampering,
> secret or open menaces, and superior skill in the manoeuvres of
> elections.[14]

Gisborne was not alone in his forebodings. When, in 1869,
the Duke of St Albans transferred the responsibility for
choosing an incumbent for the parish of Redbourne, Lincolnshire, from his own shoulders to those of a representative

group of parishioners, the prophets of doom were not slow i coming forward: 'If you give patronage to the congregation' one Conservative churchman complained, 'you will hav placards and "sandwiches" in the open streets; you will hav canvassing and trial sermons, till faith and morals, learnin and piety, are forgotten'.[15]

How far was such alarmist talk justified? Unless a parish wa lucky enough to enjoy an uncontested election with only a single nominee, canvassing was likely to take place on behal of two or more 'rival' candidates for a vacant incumbency and, human nature being what it is, such canvassing was likel sometimes to arouse strong emotions. Hopefully they could be kept within bounds. At St Peter Mancroft, one of three Norwich parishes where the incumbent was chosen by the ratepayers, elections appear to have been orderly affairs. When its vicar died in 1720, for instance, his assistant minister wa unanimously chosen to take his place; the same thing happened in 1731, when the living next fell vacant, the new assistant minister succeeding his senior without a dissentien voice. At the opposite side of the country, at Bath, the reade at the Abbey was elected rector in 1767 by the Corporation 'to the universal satisfaction both of the Inhabitants and Sojour ners'. But of course it was not always such plain sailing Thomas Wilson, the ambitious cleric of a previous chapter canvassed for six days for the lecturership of St Austin and S Faith's in the City of London. On the last day he 'waited upor most of his parishioners in both parishes'. To no avail: he wa beaten by 142 votes to 49.[16]

The doom-and-gloom brigade would no doubt have quoted the case of Painswick in Gloucestershire. The living lay in the gift of the inhabitant householders of all classes, even the poorest, and was consequently elective. 'On a recent occasion'. reported the Cotswold diarist Francis Witts in 1825, 'the place presented all the intrigue, bustle and chicanery of a contested borough; legal assessors, counsel, and attorneys, bribery, bold swearing, clamour and warm excitement'.[17] Witts's visit to Painswick obviously left a deep impression on him. Thirteen years later an Act of Parliament was passed enabling the trustees of the benefice to sell it and invest the proceeds, the dividends to be applied to diminishing the burden of poor rates in the parish. Witts thoroughly approved: 'The object has been to do away with the evil of a popular election of a vicar on each vacancy. The ratepayers having a suffrage, disorder, drunkenness and all the concommitments [sic] of a contested election, with great expense in agency, treating and the like, has hitherto been the rule of the place'. Witts wrote to his old Oxford college, Wadham, suggesting that it buy the advowson of Painswick, but Wadham declined to do so.[18] It is now in the gift of the Lord Chancellor.

One of the great parish churches of England, St Peter's, Leeds, has been in corporate patronage since 1590, when its parishioners purchased the advowson for £130 and placed it in the hands of a body of unofficial trustees. Twenty-five years later, when the living fell vacant, the trustees treated the advowson as their personal property and attempted to sell it. Their action was resisted by a strong body of parishioners, who took them to court. The result was the establishment of a statutory board of trustees.[19] On at least two occasions a contested election produced real fireworks.

The first occasion was in 1746, when a vicar of Leeds died after thirty years in the post. Two men were nominated to succeed him: Samuel Kirshaw, rector of a parish in Lincolnshire, and a local man, James Scott, incumbent of Holy Trinity, Leeds. The result of the election by the trustees was a tie: twelve votes for each candidate. Five months later Scott's supporters called a meeting at which he was elected unanimously. But his election was disputed and the matter referred to the Attorney-General, who ruled that, after four months, the right of nomination had fallen to the parishioners as a body. A parish poll was held and Kirshaw was elected. The

109

Scott camp then appealed to the Court of Chancery, which ordered a new election by the trustees. Kirshaw was again elected. He was finally instituted in March 1751, five years after the death of his predecessor.*[20]

Leeds parish church was in the news again in 1837, when another new vicar was being sought. Seven candidates were in the field (including the father of the future Lewis Carroll). The strongest was Walter Hook, vicar of Holy Trinity, Coventry, but his High Church leanings antagonized the Evangelicals of Leeds. A number of the appointing trustees went to Coventry to hear Hook preach, and were vastly impressed. 'Before the sermon', Hook said afterwards, 'they spoke of "*If* you go to Leeds"; afterwards it was "*When* you go".' One good sermon, however was insufficient in itself to silence the opposition. Arguments over Hook's churchmanship resulted in petitions and counter-petitions. Indeed, one of Hook's opponents wrote to him: 'Reverend Sir, Come not to a people that neither wish for you nor pray for you'. But Hook's advocates were equally vigorous on his behalf, and in the end he was elected by sixteen votes to seven.[22] He went on to be an outstanding vicar of Leeds and afterwards Dean of Chichester.

One of the most fascinating disputes concerning the right of parishioners to choose their own minister centred on the choice of a new perpetual curate (vicar) of Haworth, Yorkshire, in 1819. Part of its fascination stems from the fact that the principal actor in the drama was Patrick Brontë, father of the Brontë sisters. Had he failed to secure the living, as seemed

---

* His troubles were far from over. The parish of Leeds included eight chapelries, the patronage of which was a frequent source of dispute between the vicar of Leeds and the local inhabitants. At Holbeck (1754–55) Kirshaw's nominee could only obtain entry to his chapel with the help of a party of dragoons and resigned three months later. At Armley (1761–66) Kirshaw's candidate hung on to his chapelry – but only after a succession of lawsuits ending in a judgement by the Lord Chancellor.[21]

kely at one time, the sisters would have lost, with their
moorland parish, a prime source of their literary inspiration.

The dispute arose because of the peculiar nature of the
patronage of Haworth. It was in the gift of the vicar of
Bradford; but the Haworth Church Land Trustees had the
right (under a deed of 1559) to refuse the vicar's nominee. The
vicar of Bradford in 1819 was Henry Heap. He was keen to
appoint Brontë to the living, and the trustees were quite happy
to accept as their vicar a man of whom they had heard good
reports. Unfortunately Heap did the right thing in the wrong
way. Instead of humbly presenting Brontë to the trustees as his
nominee for their approval, he told them bluntly that Brontë
was to be their new incumbent. This was an insufferable blow
to their Yorkshire pride. They declined to accept Heap's
nominee. In an effort to defuse the situation Brontë rode over
to Haworth. He met one of the leading trustees, Stephen
Taylor, who advised him to resign his new appointment and to
apply for it again in two months' time – but to the trustees,
not the vicar.

This was too simple a solution. The vicar of Bradford was
disinclined to kowtow to the trustees by accepting the resignation. As Brontë reported back to Taylor: 'I should run the
greatest hazard of seriously displeasing the Archbishop, who
had received and approved my nomination'. He wavered for a
time, but, at the trustees' urging, insisted on resigning the
perpetual curacy of Haworth. The trustees were delighted. At
their request, and on the express instructions of the
Archbishop, Brontë then preached a 'trial sermon' in Haworth
church. But even this failed to break the impasse. The trustees
again informed the vicar of Bradford that they could accept
Brontë not as his nominee but only as the minister approved
by both sides. Heap, intent on saving face, declined to give
way – and instead appointed Samuel Redhead, who had been
doing duty at Haworth during the interregnum, as the new
perpetual curate.

Redhead's nomination inflamed the situation. On his fir:
Sunday as incumbent the entire congregation marched ou
during the second lesson; on his second Sunday he was howle
down; on his third Sunday he was embraced by the loca
chimney-sweep and smothered in soot. Redhead had ha
enough – and resigned.

Heap still tried to save face. He nominated three othe
clergymen in succession to the living, but the trustees refuse
all three. In the end he capitulated. He 'consented to permi
the Haworth trustees to join with him in nominating an
appointing Patrick Brontë to the cure, but, to the last, wa
assuring the Archbishop that no point of principle had bee
conceded. Brontë received his licence on 9 February 1820. Si
weeks later, on Lady Day, his youngest daughter Anne wa
christened in Haworth church. It had all been a sad muddl
Eight months had been wasted in fruitless bickerings an
attempts to save face, and in the end the candidate appointe
was the very man whom both sides to the dispute had reall
wanted all along. But at least he *had* been appointed.[23]

It was no doubt the memory of cases like these that le
Bishop Magee of Peterborough to inveigh in the House o
Lords in 1874 against the bribery, intimidation and jobber
involved in the replacement of private patronage by a syster
of popular election, 'in my opinion the very worst of a
possible modes of appointing ministers'.[24] Even Thoma
Arnold, while allowing the principle of popular election in th
case of parishes where there was no endowment and th
minister was paid by the parishioners, had thought that
candidate's qualifications should be subject to the scrutiny o
the bishop and his council: 'Never should ... the election o
the inhabitants be deemed equivalent to an actual appoin
ment'. Arnold would in fact have applied the same principle t
all forms of patronage.[25]

* * * * * * * * * *

112

There was one class of living for which Arnold's proviso would have been of no avail. This was the 'donative', a benefice which lay completely outside the jurisdiction of the diocesan bishop. Donatives were a relic of pre-Reformation times, most of them having originally been chapels of royal foundation. There were not many of them: about 100 among the 13,000 benefices of England and Wales.

The peculiar benefit of a donative for an unscrupulous patron was that he could operate without reference to higher authority. He was not required to present his nominee to the bishop for approval, so that there was no way of checking a candidate's credentials. Nor was the incumbent of a donative subject to the normal forms of episcopal visitation. The owner of a donative in the diocese of Peterborough once forbade Bishop Magee (through a lawyer's letter) to hold a confirmation in the parish church. When Magee remonstrated with him personally he replied that he had no personal feeling in the matter and would be happy to give him lunch, but that, as long as he lived, no bishop should hold a confirmation in 'his' church.[26]

The purchase of a donative was a convenient way of effecting a corrupt exchange of benefices and forcing the hand of a bishop who refused to accept a resignation, since the clergyman could hand it in direct to his patron. The acceptance of a donative automatically voided any other benefice previously held by the man presented to it. So an incumbent whose resignation the bishop for some reason was unwilling to accept could wriggle free of his benefice by getting himself appointed to a donative, which he could then resign the following day. Bishop Magee told the House of Lords in 1874 that he had heard of a donative which had been sold and resold as many as five times in a single year for this purpose.[27] In another case a clergyman accused of a crime for which the bishop wished to take proceedings against him under the Clergy Discipline Act successfully escaped prosecution by purchasing a donative in another diocese.[28]

113

Some donatives were in the hands of clerical agents wh‹ advertised sales and exchanges to be handled with 'stric‹ privacy'. Thus a clergyman who wished to resign his incum‹ bency for any reason against the wishes of his bishop had onl‹ to apply to one of these agents, who would at once refer hir‹ to the patron of a donative. The patron, for a fee of, say, £25(would grant the applicant a 'turn' of his donative, which woul‹ automatically free him from the fetters of his present living. 'I‹ one twelve-month', Magee told the Lords, 'three of the above‹ named sums were received by the patron of [the donative] fror‹ clergymen who thereby set their Ordinary at defiance. In eac‹ case the clerical agent received his ten per cent commission £25'.[29]

But there were other advantages – or evils – attached t‹ donatives. For one thing their owners were unaffected by th‹ law of 'lapse', under which the right of presentation lapse‹ from the patron to the bishop if no priest had been presente‹ to a vacant living within six months of the vacancy's arising. I‹ theory, therefore, it was possible for the owner of a donative t‹ keep a parish without a pastor for years on end – in Magee'‹ words, 'to shut the church door in the face of his parishioner‹ – and pocket the income which would otherwise have gone t‹ the incumbent. Moreover, the owner of a donative might eve‹ decline to allow an increase in the clergyman's stipend fror‹ Queen Anne's Bounty (a fund for helping the poorer clergy‹ because to have done so would have turned the donative into‹ presentative living and thus robbed him of his special privi‹ leges. So the poor priest would be kept in poverty to enable th‹ patron to hang on to his donative.[30]

Even donatives, however, had their defenders – on th‹ grounds that they were as much private property as ordinar‹ benefices. During a Lords debate in 1875 Lord Arundell c‹ Wardour, who had inherited a donative in Wiltshire, said tha‹ as a Roman Catholic he was debarred – 'very reasonably, fror‹ a Church of England point of view' – from exercising his righ‹

114

of presentation. But the donative had been purchased in 1595 by one of his ancestors, 'like any other property, in the open market'; and, if it was converted into a normal living it would be a case of simple confiscation.[31] The argument was weak, in that 'property' was here being confused with 'privilege'. It was one thing to abolish ordinary patronage without compensation: it was quite another to seek to remove such 'privileges' as the power to keep a church closed indefinitely. Donatives therefore found far fewer champions than other forms of private patronage; and not many tears were shed when they were finally abolished in 1898.

8

Absentee Shepherds

Churchgoers in the early-twenty-first-century English country side are resigned to sharing their parson with up to half dozen neighbouring parishes. Many of them count themselve lucky if they are favoured with any sort of a service in the own church every Sunday. More often than not, th overworked incumbent must rush from church to church t feed as many of his scattered faithful as possible with crumb of liturgical comfort. Usually, except where a team ministry catering for an exceptionally large area, he is labouring on h own without the benefit of a curate, and helped out only b the occasional non-stipendiary minister or lay reader. So th Anglican laity know all about the 'scandals' of moder pluralism and non-residence on the part of the clergy.

Of course the present-day 'scandals', occasioned as they ar by a shortage both of priests to minister in the parishes and c money to pay them, are very different from those of the eigh eenth and nineteenth centuries. Then the pluralism was ofte fuelled by rampant greed on the part of clergymen keen t acquire two or more stipends rather than one; non-residenc inevitably followed, as even the best-intentioned incumber was unable to live in two parsonages at once. But at least, a far as the lay sheep were concerned, the inconvenience of non-resident rector or vicar was usually mitigated to som extent by the presence of an assistant curate appointed to tak his place – at a salary infinitely less than that of his absente master. Such a system led inevitably to gross abuses. Man

116

W.E. Gladstone, Archbishop Benson's confidant on church matters.

Archbishop Tait, notorious for his bestowal of rich livings on his nearest and dearest.

ine Baring-Gould, squire as well as on at Lew Trenchard.

Leslie Paul, author of the radical 1964 report on the deployment and payment of the clergy.

William Magee, Bishop of Peterborough: he spearheaded the move for reform of the patronage system in the late nineteenth century

Edward Benson, Archbishop of Canterbury: he succeeded Magee as champion of the pro-reform movement.

parishes might still be in the care of a resident incumbent, but many were not.

The system was not without its critics. As early as 1708 Bishop Burnet of Salisbury was referring to both pluralism and non-residence as 'scandalous practices' which constituted 'so shameful a profanation of holy things' that they ought to be treated with detestation and horror.[1] A generation later another critic was castigating the practice of doing one's clerical duty by deputy: 'The plurality of benefices, because the profits of one were not sufficient to gratify [a clergyman's] avaricious desires, introduced supernumerary clergy who served as journeymen to do the work for a small stipend, while the appointed guardian of the society lived lazily and idly upon the profits of it'.[2] By 1800 Bishop Horsley of Rochester was declaring that the 'evil' of non-residence had grown to so gigantic a size that a remedy *must* be found before long.[3] And, when the subject was debated in the House of Lords in 1834, Lord Chancellor Brougham castigated the system as 'one of the greatest abuses of the Establishment – a source of weakness to it, and a never-failing ground of objection on which the enemies of the Church Establishment had been always ready to fasten'.[4]

It was one thing, however, to inveigh against an 'evil'; it was quite another to reform a system rooted in history and bestowing benefits which many of the fortunate recipients were reluctant to abandon without a struggle. From the Reformation onwards the practice of pluralism had been regulated by a statute of King Henry VIII which began well by ruling that any priest possessing a benefice worth £8 a year or more should forfeit it on his institution to any other benefice. This was fine – but its effect was to a large extent negated by a host of exceptions to the general rule. These included the sons of noblemen, royal chaplains, chaplains to both temporal and spiritual peers, university graduates and, most significantly, 'dignitaries' of the Church such as bishops,

deans and cathedral canons. All the above classes of cleri
were allowed to hold more than one living by 'dispensation'
and, since archbishops and dukes were entitled to six chaplain
each, marquesses and earls to five, viscounts and bishops t
four and even lowly barons to three each, and since Oxfor
and Cambridge graduates and Church dignitaries were thic
on the ground, the exceptions to the Henrician rule were s
numerous as to outweigh those humbler clerics who were tie
by the strict letter of the law.[5] Among the most flagran
pluralists were the bishops themselves, which made it tha
much harder for the less self-seeking among them to effect an
radical reform of the system. The Henrician statute had bee
supplemented in 1604 by a canon which laid down that, eve
where a clergyman *was* in a class permitted to hold tw
benefices, he could not do so if those benefices were 'mor
than thirty miles distant asunder'. This somewhat ambiguou
phrase was interpreted to mean a circle of forty-five statut
miles – which allowed a generous geographical spread fo
would-be pluralists. The Henrician hedge against the practic
had so many holes as to be practically useless. It was eas
enough for an ambitious cleric to find such a gap if once h
put his mind to it.

Of course the practice had its defenders. The main excus
was the poverty of the clergy. During a debate in th
Commons in 1802 Sir William Scott, a leading Church lawye
suggested that the public were not entitled to demand universa
residence on the part of the clergy when a large proportion o
the benefices in the kingdom paid so poor a salary to th
incumbent.[6] But the system could be defended on ground
other than clerical poverty. It could be claimed that the poore
parishioners would benefit more from the material ministra
tions of a wealthy pluralist than from those of a less affluen
non-pluralist. It could also be claimed that pluralism migh
well enable a busy priest to enlarge his own sphere of profes
sional activity, and that it kept in employment a large numbe

of curates who might otherwise have found themselves without a job. And, as far back as 1737, Bishop Gibson of London had argued (in a pamphlet on pluralities and non-residence) first that the pre-Reformation abuses of the system had been far greater than in subsequent centuries; secondly, that the system could be of actual advantage to the Church in the case of small livings which in themselves produced an insufficient income; and thirdly that, by allowing graduates to hold more than one living, it encouraged them to devote themselves to the serious study of divinity.[7] Certainly the system was abused less by ordinary parish priests than by senior churchmen, who acquired additional dignities at the drop of a mitre. The episcopal pot was therefore hardly in a position to blacken the character of the clerical kettle.*

A typical eighteenth-century pluralist who was also a hard-working parish priest was the writer Laurence Sterne. He held the two adjacent livings of Stillington and Sutton, Yorkshire, the latter being worth a mere £50 a year. In order to obtain the necessary dispensation he had been appointed domestic chaplain to the Earl of Aboyne, though he seems rarely, if ever, to have set eyes on his nominal lord.[9]

Some clerics even boasted of the number of livings they acquired, like an incumbent in the diocese of Exeter who, when on his deathbed, was asked by a neighbouring clergyman what use he had made of his talents:

'Use of my talents?', repeated the dying man ... 'I came into this diocese with nothing, – and now ... I am rector of

---

*A particularly flagrant offender was Archbishop Sharp of York, who helped his son to be prebendary of York, Southwell and Durham, rector of Rothbury and Archdeacon of Northumberland; and his son-in-law to be Dean of Ripon, Archdeacon of the East Riding, Master of two Ripon hospitals, prebendary of York and rector of Scrayingham: the latter also possessed a private fortune of his own and was reckoned to be the richest ecclesiastic in England.[8]

Eigncombe, worth eighty pounds; rector of Marwood, worth four hundred and fifty pounds; rector of Westcote, worth five hundred and sixty pounds; vicar of Barton, worth three hundred pounds; and rector of Eastcote, worth a thousand pounds. If that is not making use of one's talents, I do not know what is. I think I can die in peace'.[10]

Although pluralism was the principal reason for non-residence, there were others, such as ill-health or the absence of a parsonage, which were also widespread. The former was sometimes used as an excuse for idleness,* and some bishops attempted to keep it within bounds. Archbishop Secker of Canterbury, for instance, exhorted his clergy not to try their luck too blatantly, as when they complained that a particular locality might be bad for their health: 'For places called unwholesome proved upon trial very wholesome to many persons; and those which are least so must have some ministers in or near them'.[12] Secker could speak with feeling, as he had met with some hard cases during his long episcopate. In the answers to the articles of enquiry he had addressed to the clergy of the diocese of Oxford at his primary visitation in 1738 he had found plenty of excuses to arouse his suspicion. The rector of Checkinden, for instance, was claimed by his resident curate to have been for some years disabled from officiating by the gout – 'He resides in ye Summer at ye Parso-

---

* The author of *The Extraordinary Black Book* (1831) is scathing about such bogus excuses by the clergy:

They pretend sickness, in order to obtain a licence for non-residence, that they may bawl at the card-table, frequent the playhouse, tally-ho, shoot, brandish a coachman's whip, and bully at fashionable watering-places. Remember, these jovial spirits are all filled with the Holy Ghost ... that their poor curates are starving on a wretched stipend, and that, in the maintenance of both, the industrious are deprived of the fruits of their labour, and the necessary comforts of their families wasted in the profligate and dissipated lives of their parochial ministers'.[11]

nage House, but withdraws for his Health in ye Winter'.[13] Another invalid, the rector of Lillingstone Lovell, resided only 'when my health will permit, wch. in Autumn is very uncertain, by reason of a Chronical Distemper' (unspecified).[14] Secker must have been equally sceptical of some of the claims made for unsuitable parsonages – like the vicar of Headington's vague excuse that 'ye vicaridge is not, of itself, good enough to support its Vicar'.[15] He would have been more impressed by the devotion to duty of the curate of Stratton Audley: 'In Winter (My Lord) I constantly reside – 'tho with some Difficulty, being obliged to dress my Victuals in my Bed Chamber'.[16]

The excuses for non-residence put forward in answer to Secker's enquiries were not restricted to ill-health and unsuitable parsonages. Some absentee clerics were airily nonchalant: like the vicar of Mapledurham, who explained his occasional absences as being due to his necessary visits to Eton College, of which he happened to be a fellow;[17] or the rector of Newnham Courtnay, who resided 'sometime in Bath, and sometime with my Friends by London';[18] or the vicar of Shirburn, who resided constantly 'except when I attend Ld. Macclesfield's Family in London' (Macclesfield was the local squire);[19] or the rector of Swincombe, who 'removed wth. my family to Oxford for the advantage of education for my children', his curate 'takeing care of any weekly duties that shd. happen at Swyncomb'.[20]

The replies of others were whimsical, if not downright peculiar, and cast a fascinating light on the human foibles of the eighteenth-century English clergy. Thus the rector of Heythrop with Little Rollright, after explaining that there had never been 'in the memory of man' any house or glebe belonging to either benefice and that he therefore resided at Chipping Norton two miles away, complains about the bishop's requirement of a Sunday-morning service at Heythrop:

The people of Little Rollright respect me for my service; and have lately adorned ye pulpit for me in a handsome manner. But to be torn away from Them, and sent on a Sunday morning to Heathrop, to read to the Church-walls (wch. I am sure would be the case, the Clerk only excepted): this, my Lord, is to me a melancholy consideration. Out of the whole of 7 houses of fixed inhabitants those that are called Church-goers, only two men; the Clerk one, who is forced to be Churchwarden; and two old women, who are very infirm ... Nor will reading to the walls be the worst of the case. I am already forced to be obliged to the Papist at Heathrop for a Stable. If I am sent thither in a morning, I must either fast (wch. will put me into a fever) or be obliged to him likewise for a dinner ... That will draw on me something of an acquaintance; and that acquaintance will draw me upon a fresh censure of *countenancing Popery*.[21]

Perhaps the most tantalizingly discreet answer of all came from the rector of Stoke Talmage to excuse his living a mile and a half outside his parish 'with the knowledge of His Grace the Lord Archbishop of Canterbury, as well as of my patrons the Earl of Macclesfield and Lord Carteret'. The reply concludes: 'If your Lordship is desirous to know my Reasons, I shall be ready to wait upon You whenever You please, some of my Reasons being of a Nature not proper to be put into Writing'.[22]

About the same time as Bishop Secker was probing into the state of the parishes of the diocese of Oxford, Archbishop Thomas Herring was conducting a similar enquiry among the clergy of the diocese of York. The returns reveal that, in 1743 393 parishes there had non-resident parsons out of a total of 836 (excluding York itself). The corresponding figures for Oxford in 1738 were 79 non-residents out of a total of 179 (the diocese was then confined to Oxfordshire).

The York answers to the question on non-residence include a similar crop of often shameless excuses and of intriguing oddities. Sometimes the needs of the aristocracy are required to take precedence over the needs of the parish. The rector of

Ashton, for instance, resides constantly upon his cure 'except when my Attendance is required as Domestick Chaplain to the Earl of Holdernesse'.[23] Sometimes educational needs are paramount. The vicar of Easingwold resides by dispensation at Manchester, 'where I am entrusted with ye Education of a few Young Gentlemen'.[24] The vicar of Easington, another permanent non-resident by permission of Herring's predecessor, has removed to Hull in order to be 'under the Instruction of my Uncle, who is the Lecturer of Hull'.[25]

Some clerics have qualms of conscience at being away from their parishes – like the rector of Londesborough, who was allowed by the previous archbishop to be excused residence 'on account of my being usefull in the Cathedral wherento I belong. But as I think it would be an unreasonable request to desire to be farther indulged, I have taken my measures for quitting my other preferments and resideing constantly'.[26] And the rector of Kirkby Misperton sneaks in a splendid commercial for his aristocratic hero: 'I have been personally resident upon my Cure upwards of thirtysix years, excepting about five years that I served in Flanders as Chaplain under three successive Colonels ... in the glorious times of the invincible and successful Duke of Marlborough, who never fought a battle but what he won and prov'd decisive, nor ever besieged a Town but what he took'.[27]

One cleric who had attempted to cut his coat far beyond his cloth was the rector of Craythorne. He threw himself unashamedly on the mercy of his diocesan:

I've been Rectr. of this living upwards of Twenty seven years, and Resident all the time except Seven years which was occasioned by building a Spacious Parsonage House and thereby Involved my self so far that I was forced to sell my living to answer my Credit and Shift for my support all that time and am not even with the world yet which I beg your Grace would be Pleased to consider whenever you've favours to bestow and the rather that I'm the Oldest Rectr. in Cleveland.[28]

123

And one who thought his deputy's needs greater than his own (or maybe disliked young children *en masse*) was the non-resident rector of Stanford: 'The Curate resides in ye Parsonage House and being A married Man having A child every year and now six living there is not convenience for me to make use of a Room and Furniture wch. I reserv'd for that purpose'.[29]

In some parishes where the incumbent is non-resident the answers are supplied by the curate. At Flamborough, for instance, 'the proper Incumbent is an old craz'd Man and resides at Hornsea'.[30] At Kirkby Moorside 'The Vicar resides at London' (he was also a canon of Lichfield).[31] At Cowsby the rector 'is indisposed at Birmingham with his Relations'.[32] At Kirk Bramwith the rector had forsaken the living ten years previously 'on account of a great many large debts contracted by him when he was resident upon his Cure'.[33] But occasionally an absentee incumbent speaks up for himself, like the pluralist vicar of Kirk Burton, whose curate had written to him to say that his parishioners were complaining about his absence: 'Methinks Yorkshire nettles are very forward this summer and sting mightily … the people grumble and upbraid you with my absence? Silly people for so doing. How can you help it?'[34]

One could go on quoting *ad infinitum*, but these samples from two sets of diocesan returns indicate something of the scale of non-residence in mid-eighteenth-century England and of the particular reasons for it. There is no reason to suppose that the problem was vastly different in other English dioceses.

* * * * * * * * * *

As the eighteenth century advanced, attacks on pluralism, with its necessary accompaniment of non-residence, became more vocal. At the turn of the century Thomas Gisborne, a prebendary of Durham, was exhorting the bishops to refrain from bestowing two livings on the same man if either living could support a minister of its own. 'It is certainly true',

Gisborne conceded, 'that a Clergyman distinguished for active piety might frequently be of more service to religion *individually* by having two parishes committed to his care than he would have been with only one'. But a greater service would be rendered to religion by offering the second parish to the best of the unbeneficed clergy known to the bishop.[35]

Some bishops heeded Gisborne's advice to the extent of attempting to stem the pluralistic tide, or at least to keep it within bounds. Archbishop Secker, in the mid-eighteenth century, was unable to prohibit pluralism altogether because many livings in his diocese were so poor, but he endeavoured to reduce its incidence. He exhorted his clergy to remember their pastoral responsibilities, and not to pretend that it was perfectly in order to fob their parishioners off with a curate. In one of his charges he warned them that they were bound to ensure not merely that their parochial duties were performed but that they personally should perform them: 'If it were enough to substitute another to do them, a layman would be in point of conscience and reason as capable of holding a benefice as a man in holy orders'.[36] An earlier archbishop, Tenison, had endeavoured at least to keep to the letter of the law by ensuring that, where a dispensation was granted to hold two benefices, the benefices were no more than the legal maximum of thirty miles apart. He protested to Queen Anne in 1713 against a proposed royal dispensation to a pluralist to hold two benefices outside the canonical distance. In the case of applicants who applied to him for his own dispensation he instituted a rigorous enquiry before agreeing to grant it. The would-be pluralists were required to show a high standard of learning and to undergo a written examination.[37]

A century later the situation was as bad or worse, but the problem was how to grapple with it. It could best be tackled locally by a strong-minded reforming diocesan. Such a bishop was Henry Phillpotts of Exeter. His vast diocese covered the whole of Devon and Cornwall; and, at the beginning of his reign in 1831, one in every ten of its parishes lacked a resident minister. But Phillpotts was prepared to see the matter in proportion. He would issue stern warnings to notorious non-residents, while accepting that in some cases a clergyman was doing his duty satisfactorily though living just outside the boundaries of his parish (in modern parlance a 'virtual resident') and that in other cases the population of a parish might be too small to justify a resident minister. And, in the course of his charge to his diocese in 1836, he emphasized that he had insisted on residence 'in every case in which it appeared to me consistent with justice or fitness to enforce it'. In the same charge he pointed out the improvement that had already taken place in the diocese. At the time of his primary visitation in 1833 there had been seventy parishes without a resident minister; this number had now been reduced to forty-nine. So his strictures were obviously taking effect.[38]

Similar success attended the efforts of Bishop Charles James Blomfield of London,* who spearheaded moves for reforming the Church. According to the official returns for 1827, there were then 255 resident incumbents serving the 577 benefices in his diocese. By 1831 the number of residents had risen to 287, by 1835 to 325 and by 1838 to 409.[39]

In some cases non-residence was of such a scandalous nature that even the most reactionary or spineless bishop was obliged to take note of it. Such a case was that of an absentee rector of Eversley, Hampshire, John Tooley-Hawley, who, after neglecting his parochial duties in favour of his more attractive female parishioners, fled to the Continent to avoid the atten-

---

* Blomfield's reputation was such that Sydney Smith observed in a pamphlet 'When the Church of England is mentioned it will only mean *Charles James of London*, who will enjoy a greater power than has ever been possessed by any Churchman since the days of Laud'.[40] And Archbishop Vernon Harcourt of York, a colleague on the newly-formed Ecclesiastical Commission (a brainchild of Blomfield's), remarked: 'Till Blomfield comes we all sit and mend our pens and talk about the weather'.[41]

tions both of irate husbands and of the Church authorities. In spite of repeated demands from the Bishop of Winchester to explain if not excuse his actions, he kept silent – and the living was eventually deemed to be vacant.[42] It was bestowed by its patron on Charles Kingsley, who had previously served in the parish as a curate and had endeared himself to the villagers. He was to prove equally successful as their rector.

Occasionally the full rigour of the law was invoked against incumbents who, far from being notorious evil-livers, performed their parochial duties with blameless competence but fell foul of the authorities through being technically non-resident without the necessary dispensation. A case mentioned in the Commons in 1802 by Sir William Scott, when introducing his Clergy Non-Residence Bill, was that of a former rector of Bow, in the East End of London. He had proved an exemplary clergyman who had performed his duties in an 'assiduous and edifying manner'. The prosecution, said Scott, had admitted that for this very reason he had been selected for the purpose of showing that no merit could excuse the legal guilt of non-residence, since he lived not in the parish of Bow itself but in the neighbouring parish of St Andrew, Holborn. He had migrated there simply because the parsonage at Bow was so poky and uncomfortable as to be virtually uninhabitable. Nevertheless, it *could* have been lived in; and the jury therefore found for the full penalties against the defendant.[43] Presumably the authorities had brought the prosecution in order to deter less admirable incumbents from illegal non-residence. But it was bad luck on the blameless rector of Bow.

This was not the only case of its kind to be aired in Parliament. Twice in the early months of 1834 specific cases of pluralism and non-residence came up for debate. The first concerned the parish of Allhallows, Lombard-street, London, whose parishioners had presented a petition to Parliament objecting to the appointment of the Rev. Francis Dawson to the benefice, on the ground that he was already rector of

Chislehurst, rector of Orpington, and prebendary and sub-dean of Canterbury Cathedral. The living was in the gift of the Dean and Chapter of Canterbury – who, in the opinion of the petitioners, had been guilty of the 'most lamentable abuse of the patronage of the Church'. They had nothing against Mr Dawson personally; they were aware of his excellent character and irreproachable conduct; but they contended that, whatever his merits or demerits might be, his non-residence among them put those merits totally beyond their reach. In a rhetorical flourish they stressed the 'increasing dissatisfaction of the people of England on account of so large a portion of the clergy of the Established Church holding a plurality of livings and residing at a distance from them'. In defence of Dawson (who was a former chaplain of the House of Commons) it was argued both in the Lords and in the Commons that the Dean and Chapter of Canterbury were bound by statute to offer livings within their gift to members of the chapter and that, in effect, it had been Dawson's turn for preferment. Although the petition, in parliamentary parlance, had simply been 'laid on the table', the opportunity to debate the general issues of pluralism and non-residence had increased the public awareness that here was an aspect of the Church set-up that was ripe for reform.[44]

The public was given a further opportunity to hear about the alleged evils of non-residence when the Christchurch (Surrey) Rectory Bill came up in the Commons for its second reading. This case was less straightforward than that of Allhallows, in that the rector concerned was absent for only three months of the year (the permitted maximum) in his second parish of Mitcham – but was technically always non-resident because he lived six doors outside his main parish of Christchurch (another case, surely, of 'virtual residence'). The rector, a father of eight, received only £112 (from tithes) after paying his curate, but was required to serve a parish of 13,000 souls. He had formerly received a much larger stipend from the voluntary contributions of his parishioners, but they had been persuaded to discontinue that support on the ground of his 'non-residence'. The Bill before the House sought to convert the voluntary payment into a compulsory parish rate of £400 a year.

The Bill excited strenuous opposition among MPs, on the grounds that the rector spent too much time outside the parish and that it was entirely wrong to levy a compulsory rate on parishioners of whatever religious persuasion in order to bump up his income to the level considered necessary for his maintenance in his proper station (or, as one speaker put it, 'sufficient to support a gentleman'). The opposition was to some extent bogus, in that the rector, though technically 'non-resident', lived only 400 yards from his parish church, had laboured tirelessly in Christchurch for the past twenty-five years, and was holding the living of Mitcham only until such time as a would-be cleric, currently a minor, was old enough to take charge. But it was sufficiently vocal to secure the defeat of the Bill by forty-one votes (thirty-three Ayes, seventy-four Nos). And the impassioned speeches on either side ensured that pluralism and non-residence were kept in the public eye and that any attempt to reform them would gain a certain measure of support.[45]

* * * * * * * * * *

What was the proportion of resident to non-resident clergy in the eighteenth and nineteenth centuries? A precise picture is hard to come by, in the absence of unimpeachable statistics. But a rough idea of the situation may be reached by an examination of such diocesan returns and other official or semi-official sources as are available.

The fullest analysis for eighteenth-century England is that made by Peter Virgin in *The Church in an Age of Negligence*. By probing the returns made for Queen Anne's Bounty in 1705 by four dioceses in different parts of the country he concludes, first, that there was comparatively little plurality in early-eighteenth-century England and, secondly, that such as did exist was evenly distributed. Some of the 1705 pluralists, however, appear to have been pluralists only in name. Thus, according to his archdeacon, the perpetual curate of Woodbury, Devon, 'has another living, to wit Sidmouth, but he receives no benefit from it, giving the profits of it to the widow of the last Incumbent'.[46] Such an example of generosity gives the lie to those who contend that clerical pluralism was invariably associated with self-interest. Nor, in those parts of England where pluralism *was* widespread, was it necessarily harmful in its effects. In the archdeaconry of Stow in the diocese of Lincoln pluralism appears to have been nearly universal; but the livings were grouped in such a way, and the benefices and curacies were so interrelated, as to give parishes as many church services as possible[47] (in some ways anticipating the modern group ministry).

By the closing quarter of the eighteenth century, however, pluralism was on the increase. In 1705 only 16 per cent of the beneficed clergy were pluralists, but by 1775 this figure had risen to 36 per cent. This increase may have been partly due to a fall in the number of ordinands – a situation paralleled in today's Church. By the early nineteenth century the rise in pluralism, the main cause of non-residence, had led to a resultant rise in absenteeism. The parliamentary returns for 1813 show that, out of 10,558 parishes in England and Wales which submitted returns, only 4,183, or 40 per cent, were served by resident incumbents.[48] This was bad enough, but it was made worse by the fact that by no means all the parishes lacking a resident incumbent were served by a deputy in the shape of a curate. The Commissioners' Report of 1835 reckoned that 4,224 of the 5,230 curates in England and Wales were employed by non-resident incumbents. As the number of non-residents revealed by the 1827 returns had been no fewer than 6,120, it is likely that about 2,000 parishes, or one in every six or seven, lacked a resident clergyman of any sort.[49] This statistic contrasts with that quoted by *The Extraordinary Black Book* in its report on the findings of a certain Mr Wright, a former secretary to the Bishops of London, Norwich and Ely, given in a letter (one of a series) published in the *Morning Chronicle* (20 November 1813). Wright had claimed that as many as 4,788 benefices had neither a resident incumbent nor a resident curate and consequently had to be served by neighbouring clerics. In one diocese, said Wright, one-third of the livings had only one service each Sunday instead of two, and in another diocese one-third of the parsonage houses had been described as being in a bad state of repair 'as an excuse for the non-residence of our gentlemen pastors'. Wright backed up his general statistics with some colourful examples of clerics who worked the system to their own advantage. One incumbent, he alleged, held two valuable rectories worth £1,200 per annum, to obtain which he had promised the archbishop that he would constantly reside on one and keep a resident curate on the other, himself preaching thirteen times a year on the benefice where he did not reside. 'This worthy son of the church contrived to evade these conditions, and got a poor devil of a curate to do the work of both livings for £84 a year'.[50]

Admittedly the militant Wright had an axe to grind, in that he claimed to have suffered financial losses in the service of his right reverend employers; but his findings were defended by the anonymous author of the *Black Book* as being in line with the diocesan returns laid before the Privy Council:

> The clergy were terribly alarmed at his disclosures: they resorted to every artifice to avert the storm, and save their pockets ... lies and calumnies of every shape and description were vomited forth to blacken the character of Mr Wright; he was stigmatized as an 'informer' who, availing himself of his official situation, was in part the cause of and then the betrayer of their guilt.[51]

Allowing for a certain element of exaggeration on the part of both Wright and the author of the *Black Book*, their charges were sufficiently near the bone to alarm not a few eminent ecclesiastics and to add impetus to the process of reform.

Plurality and non-residence were not specific abuses of the patronage system as such. But they were part and parcel of the system. The way in which the system worked encouraged the growth of pluralism in that, if a powerful patron liked a particular cleric, he would seek to reward him with more than one benefice. So, when it came to reforming patronage, it was hard to do so without at the same time tackling the linked abuses of pluralism and non-residence. How that reform took shape will be the subject of our next chapter.

9

One Step at a Time

The long process of parliamentary reform of the patronage system got underway with Sir William Scott's Clergy Non-Residence Bill of 1802. The Bill, which became law the following year, had as its twin aims the legalization and regularization of non-residence. Under the terms of the Act any incumbent not wishing to reside in his benefice had first to obtain the consent of his bishop. Exemptions from residence could be obtained for such reasons as 'ill-health' or 'residence on another living'; but, without his bishop's licence, an incumbent was breaking the law if he continued non-resident and risking the forfeiture of the income of his living.

Many bishops were slow in chasing up their absentee clerics. One diocesan, Hurd of Worcester, even went so far as to admit in 1807 that he had ceased to enforce the laws against non-residence 'because they caused such inconvenience'. Another, Carey of Exeter, declined to order two of his incumbents who resided in Malaya and Brazil to return to their respective parishes of Dittisham and Honeychurch.[1] But, at least in theory, the rules against non-residence had been tightened up. Moreover, the Act attempted to regularize the situation still further by requiring each bishop to send a return to the Privy Council of the number of parishes in his diocese lacking a resident incumbent. These returns were then collated and presented to Parliament, which was thus enabled to keep tabs on the situation.

Part of the trouble, of course, concerned the relative poverty of the clergy. Many cases of non-residence, as has been seen arose from the fact that the priest in question was holding more than one living. And, as Scott* observed when introducing his Bill in the Commons, 'how can the public demand under pains and penalties, that there shall be a resident incumbent in each parish when so large a proportion of the benefices in the kingdom do not pay more than what most of us in this House pay to our upper servants?'[2]

A subsidiary purpose of Scott's Bill was to help the poorer clergy by repealing a statute of King Henry VIII which, among other things, hindered a priest from farming his glebe as effectively as possible. Even such a modest aim led one critic of the Bill to ask whether they wanted to see the clergy turned into farmers who would retail corn, turnips and potatoes to their parishioners instead of the 'pure and wholesome milk of the gospel'.[3]

* * * * * * * * * *

The country had to wait a quarter of a century before the next significant move. This was the Clergy Resignation Bonds Act of 1828, popularly known as the 'Warming-Pan Act'. Its purpose, in the words of the Solicitor-General who introduced it, was simply to 'render legal that which is now practised in defiance of the law'. What lay behind the Act was a decision by the House of Lords in 1827 that a bond to resign a living in favour of the patron's brother was illegal. Many patrons and incumbents felt themselves endangered by this decision and facing possible prosecution for simony. So the Archbishop of Canterbury, Manners Sutton, hurriedly introduced a Bill into Parliament validating all such agreements which had been made in the past.

---

* Sir William Scott, later Baron Stowell (1745–1836), was a distinguished judge as well as an MP, specializing in maritime and ecclesiastical law. He was appointed Vicar-General for the province of Canterbury in 1788.

A further Bill, passed the following year, legalized such bonds for the future – but only if they were made out in favour of near relations by blood or marriage. Both Bills were brought in to mollify the patrons as a body – and were a surrender to *force majeure*, as the Solicitor-General more or less admitted: 'The intention of this Bill is to enable the holders of benefices [i.e., patrons], whether lay or clerical, to provide for their families as they are enabled to do with other species of property'. It was better, he added, to make legal and above-board that which would otherwise be managed clandestinely or by the 'detestable expedient' of appointing the aged or the dying to livings which it was desired to leave vacant as soon as possible.[4] A Bill so beneficial to patrons had no difficulty in securing the approval of a parliament many of whose members were patrons themselves. Nearly half a century later it was denounced by Bishop Magee of Peterborough in no uncertain terms. But it was not until the end of the century that resignation bonds were finally declared illegal.

The process of general Church reform which got under way in the 1830s and led to the formation of the Ecclesiastical Commissioners soon caught up patronage – or, more particularly, pluralism – in its net. The first attempts to get the system under control – two Bills introduced in the Lords in 1831 and 1832* by Archbishop Manners Sutton's successor, William Howley – were abortive, however. Both Bills included a clause prohibiting incumbents from accepting a second living if the first was worth more than £400 a year, but weakened the effect of the prohibition by allowing exemptions to Masters of Arts.

---

* During one of the debates in the Lords on the 1832 Bill a peer drew attention to an advertisement offering for sale the advowson of a Norfolk living, worth £650 a year, the church of which was stated to have 'gone to sea'. 'The sea had made considerable encroachments on many parts of the coast of Norfolk, and the land on which this church stood was now under water. The value of this living was, therefore, enhanced by the circumstance of there being no church and ... a total absence of any duties to perform'.[5]

Six years later a new Pluralities Bill survived its passage through both Lords and Commons and became law. The resultant Act of 1838 – its full title was 'An Act to Abridge the Holding of Benefices in Plurality and to make Better Provision for the Residence of the Clergy' – put a stop both to excessive pluralism and to excessive incomes for pluralists. Incumbents were restricted to a maximum of two benefices, the maximum aggregate value of which could not exceed £1,000 a year. A further restriction was put on pluralists by the requirement that, where two livings *were* held by the same man, they must be under ten statute miles apart instead of under thirty miles as hitherto. The purpose of the ten-mile limit was to ensure that a pluralist incumbent lived near enough to that one of his two livings where he did *not* reside to ensure its adequate supervision by a curate. The number of clergymen affected by the other provisions of the Act was comparatively few, since only 6 per cent held three livings or more and only 5 per cent received stipends in excess of £1,000 a year. Life-interests were respected, so no radical changes were effected immediately. But at least Parliament had gone some way towards tackling a glaring abuse in the Church and ensuring that pastoral interests as well as property interests were protected.

It had gone some way; but, in the opinion of the more radical critics of the system, it had not gone nearly far enough. One MP during a Commons debate on the Bill described pluralism as 'an insult to common sense and common justice; a corrupt perversion and appropriation of the Church revenue from the object for which it was assigned; it is vicious in principle and destructive in practice'. Not surprisingly this critic thought the Bill grossly inadequate in allowing a clergyman, by taking a second living,

> to become a mere spectator in spiritual service, a contractor for the supply of religious instruction by means of a mercenary substitute which he may provide at the lowest price at which

136

such can be obtained in the Church market, pocketing, for the gratification of his own cupidity, the difference in amount between ... the price received from the parish and the pittance paid to his hireling jobber [i.e., the curate].[6]

Such criticisms were of course balanced by others suggesting that the reforms proposed were far too radical. In the end the Act represented a judicious compromise which cut pluralism down to size and ironed out its more flagrant abuses.

Its effects were reinforced by the Pluralities Act of 1850, which reduced the permitted distance between churches which might be held jointly from ten miles to three by the nearest country road.* By then the proportion of parishes with resident incumbents was on the increase, and the rise continued steadily over the next thirty years. By 1879 the number of parishes in England and Wales with resident incumbents was 11,186 – nearly 90 per cent of the total. The comparable figure in 1850 had been a little under 70 per cent.[8] (A century later the process was going into reverse as a growing shortage of clergy led to more and more livings being held in plurality with others. By the 1990s groups of four or five parishes in the care of a single priest were commonplace and, in the countryside at least, non-residence the rule rather than the exception. But that is another story!)

* * * * * * * * * *

Pluralism had been curbed by the Acts of 1838 and 1850, and non-residence consequently grew less and less common. Patronage itself was a much tougher proposition; and it took many years of parliamentary in-fighting for its wings to be clipped. Between 1870 and 1898 no fewer than twenty-five Bills dealing with various aspects of the problem were introduced in

---

*A necessary proviso. As Bishop Frederick Temple retorted to an aspiring pluralist cleric who had remarked how near his two churches were to each other 'as the crow flies': 'Yer not a crow and yer can't fly'.[7]

either the Lords or the Commons, but almost all fell by the wayside.

The first move came in 1870, when R. Assheton (later Viscount) Cross, a moderate High Churchman, and the Evangelical Lord Sandon introduced a Bill to abolish the sale of next presentations. It was a modest little Bill which sought also to abolish sales with secret conditions and sales transacted 'at a time when the incumbent is by reason of sickness in extreme danger of death'.* The Bill passed the Commons without a division, but was opposed in the Lords as an infringement of property rights and was allowed to lapse. The following year a joint committee of the Convocations of Canterbury and York advocated a ban on the sale of next presentations.

By now a considerable opposition to the existing patronage system was growing up in the Church at large. The commercial market in livings, in the words of Bishop Temple of Exeter, was a 'shock to the religious feeling of a great number of people, especially the artisan class and the lower middle class', and represented a 'stumbling-block greater than it is quite easy for more educated people to measure'.[10] To many of the bishops it was clear that something had to be done. Temple himself was among the foremost advocates of change. He considered the patronage system the greatest external hindrance to the well-being of the parochial ministry and would like to have seen the total abolition of the sale of livings. But it was a fellow diocesan, Magee of Peterborough, who spearheaded the movement for reform.

Magee, who had been Dean of Cork before his consecration,

---

* The Bill was intended specifically to meet the circumstances of cases like the recent *Fox* v. *the Bishop of Chester*. Here the patron concerned completed the sale of an advowson in the afternoon, the incumbent died the same evening, and the cleric who had bought the advowson took immediate possession. He had the protection of the courts, and the bishop was compelled to institute him.[9]

had made a name for himself as one of the greatest orators of the day. Queen Victoria thought him 'the finest preacher the Queen has ever heard out of Scotland', though Disraeli was less enthusiastic: 'His judgment cannot be relied on', he told the Queen when opposing Magee's translation to Durham. 'He is vehement in opposite directions; and, above all, he is wanting in dignity of manner and mind'.[11] Whatever his possible shortcomings, however, Magee's oratorical prowess made him an ideal candidate for raising the banner of reform in the Lords. (The then Archbishop of Canterbury, Tait, was ruled out because of the notorious way in which he promoted his own relatives to the best livings in his gift.)* He was able to put the case against the existing system as one who cared nothing for patronage himself. 'God knows, and He only, how I hate patronage', he once wrote to his friend and future biographer, J.C. MacDonnell. 'It is the most anxious, thankless, and disappointing duty that any man can be called on to perform. He is certain to disappoint nineteen out of twenty eligible men, and then it is twenty to one that the twentieth disappoints *him*'.[13]

Magee's opportunity came in 1874, with the defeat of Gladstone's first government and the return of the Conservatives to power under Disraeli. It seemed to Magee an ideal moment for proposing some modest reforms. The Conservative Party was traditionally better disposed to the Church than the Liberals, and he had the offer of government support. He began in a small way: by moving in the House of Lords for a select committee on Church patronage. His aim, he told the

---

*Magee had a low opinion of Tait, of whom he wrote in 1876: 'He so entirely believes in Parliament, and so entirely ignores the clergy, that he is really becoming, with all his noble qualities and great practical sagacity, a great peril to the Church. He regards the clergy as a big Sixth Form [Tait had once been headmaster of Rugby], and the outer world as the parents and trustees of the big school, the Church, and acts accordingly'.[12]

139

Lords, was to give the Church an opportunity to rid itself of the stigma of 'trafficking' in livings. The deep-seated evil in the system was that patronage had come to be regarded too much as a property and too little as a trust. Magee's speech was immensely long and detailed. He was supported by the Lord Chancellor, Earl Cairns, who agreed on behalf of the government to the appointment of a select committee, thus precluding further debate.

Magee was under no illusions about the difficulty of his task. Even before the debate he reported to MacDonnell that, in a preliminary discussion at the Athenaeum with Cairns and the Duke of Richmond, he had found the two peers, though 'amiable' and quite willing to assent to the committee, 'a little nervous as to the "extent" of my motion'.[14] Three days later he wrote:

> I find everyone very nervous about the subject, and awfully afraid of any damage to 'property'. They do not yet see that identifying property with nuisances is not the best way to preserve it. But I shall certainly have a very difficult card to play between speaking so as not to offend Conservative lords who are large patrons, and speaking so as not to offend the conscience of the Church by a bishop palliating gross abuse.[15]

In the event Magee won the first round without difficulty, and the select committee was appointed.

The committee deliberated over the next few months and brought forward a series of proposals for a moderate reform of the existing system. It expressed a desire that all legislation affecting Church patronage 'should proceed upon the principle that patronage is a trust, to be exercised for the spiritual benefit of the parishioners'. With the aid of the parliamentary draftsmen Magee put together a Bill based on the committee's recommendations. It was an uphill task. 'I go to town on Monday to discuss my Patronage Bill with the draftsman and with [the Archbishop of York]', he told MacDonnell; 'then will

ome [the Archbishop of Canterbury], Selborne, and Cairns;
hen the Bishops, at Lambeth; then the House of Lords; then
he Commons. By the time it gets through all these sieves, if it
ver does, it may come out like "the little end of nothing
whittled down to a point"'.[16] Five days later he was
omplaining to MacDonnell: 'Every foolish peer and member
f Parliament will have a chance of grafting his little bit of
olly into the Bill, and what we shall get in the end, if we get
nything, heaven only knows'.[17]

The Bill, in its final draft, proposed to make it lawful for a
ishop to refuse to institute a priest if he had not been in
oly orders for three years, was over 70 years old or was
unable from bodily infirmity adequately to perform the
uties of the benefice'. It authorized any three or more
arishioners (defined, in sexist terms, as 'male persons of full
ge') to enter a caveat within fourteen days stating the
rounds on which they objected to the institution; the matter
vould then be determined either by the bishop or (failing the
onsent of all parties) by the judge appointed under the new
ublic Worship Regulation Act, from whom an appeal lay to
he Judicial Committee of the Privy Council. Both patron
nd priest were required to make a declaration against
imony much more precise than that enacted in 1865 (which
ad itself replaced the oath against simony required by the
anon of 1604); if the declaration proved false, the guilty
arty was to be 'prosecuted, deemed guilty of a misdemea-
our (if convicted), and punished accordingly' (exactly *how*
vas not specified). As the select committee, by a majority of
ne, had declined to condemn the sale of next presentations,
hese were not dealt with in the Bill. But it dipped its toe in
he water by forbidding a cleric who had purchased the
dvowson of a benefice (either in his own name or acting
hrough trustees) to be instituted until the *second* vacancy or
he expiration of ten years after such purchase, whichever
hould happen first. This was intended to prevent the repre-

141

hensible but common practice of a priest's buying an advowson, presenting himself, and then selling the advowson as soon as he wanted to move elsewhere.

The Bill attempted to introduce a modest measure of reform into a system which, in the opinion of the select committee, left much to be desired. But, even so, it proposed too much for Parliament to swallow. It was introduced into the Lords on 25 February 1875 and survived its second reading. Magee was not sanguine about its chances thereafter: 'What a deal of coaxing and earwigging it has taken me to get even so far', he reported to MacDonnell, 'and still I have all the breakers and rocks of Committee ahead'.[18] He was not helped by some of his allies – notably Temple, who raised many hackles by advocating a veto on all sales of livings: 'The Bishop of Exeter's speech greatly displeased the Conservative peers. It was thought very revolutionary ... making my proposals seem moderate by comparison'.[19]

By late March Magee was reporting the Bill's prospects as 'not encouraging – cold support from friends, and active opposition from vested interests'. Its bitterest foes turned out to be the clerical patrons, 'who are, as the clergy so generally are, given to panics, and incapable of seeing outside the edges of their own parishes ... The result of this false Conservatism will be ecclesiastical revolution. Suppressed reform is like suppressed gout – sure to fly to the heart at last; and then *exeunt omnes*'.[20] Magee soldiered on, however, at the committee stage of his Bill. 'Cairns and Richmond are behaving *very* fairly', he told MacDonnell, 'not at all cushioning or obstructing the Bill, but honestly trying to improve it according to their lights – and, in some respects decidedly doing so according to mine'.[21]

Magee became more and more incensed against the priestly opponents of the Bill. 'Clerical patrons are acting very unwisely for their own interests in opposing the whole Bill so bitterly as they are doing', he complained to MacDonnell:

They will never have a milder one, that is certain. The longer they delay the Bill, the longer they keep up the agitation on the subject, and so continually depreciate the selling value of their own property ... The result will be, sooner or later, that men will not preserve the abuse for the sake of the property, but get rid of the property in order to get rid of the abuse. Certainly nothing can well be more damaging to the Church than the fact – if it turn out to be a fact – of the existence of such a blue book of damaging facts and evidences as last year's report of my committee, and the fact that all reform of these was stopped by the clergy of the Church. But the clergy in a panic are like horses in a stampede – nothing will hold them.[22]

But it was not only the clergy who were to blame. A rash of pamphlets had been rushed out in denunciation of the Bill. And, at a public meeting, the bishops were accused of sponsoring 'a confiscation of the property of the lay patrons ... such as the wildest denominationalist never dreamt of'.[23]

The Bill survived both its committee stage and its third reading and went down to the Commons, in Magee's words, 'with fairly flying colours'.[24] But there it foundered, mainly because Magee could find no MP willing to risk the wrath of so many parliamentary patrons by piloting it through the House. When his last hope – Spencer Walpole, the MP for Cambridge University – threw in the towel he gave vent to his feelings in an impassioned lament to MacDonnell: 'I had a letter from Walpole lately, renouncing charge of my Bill, *avowedly* because it allows parishioners a voice in the selecting of pastors, which it does not, only a right of objecting on defined grounds, and secondly, because it interferes with sales of advowsons and presentations, with which it in no way meddles'.[25]

The real reason for Walpole's withdrawal, in Magee's view, was fear of his clerical constituents:*

* Walpole (1806–98) had good reason to fear the public. A former Home Secretary, he had been driven from office by popular clamour in May 1867

Really and truly the conduct of the clergy on this question is very discreditable. The reform of patronage which they really want is one in the interest of the *clerical order*, securing better *promotion*, not one in the interests of the parishioners or the Church, securing better *men*. I am very sick of the whole thing. The editor of the *Guardian* is privately urgent with me to 'go on' ... But how am I to 'go on' when I can get no man to take up the question in the Commons; and when it would be obviously absurd to re-introduce the Bill in the Lords?[26]

Magee bowed to the inevitable, and his Bill sank without trace

* * * * * * * * * *

The next move was a notorious delaying tactic: the appoint ment by the government in 1878 of a royal commission on the 'sale, exchange and resignation of ecclesiastical benefices'. The commission's report, when it came out the following year, wa packed with juicy examples of the kind of scandal which it wa desired to remedy; but its conclusions were much the same a those of the select committee of 1874. The existing system wa approved in principle: 'The varied system of patronage, publi and private, interests all classes and ensures the representatior of different views'. So the commissioners concentrated thei efforts on seeking to remedy a few gross abuses. A bishop, fo instance, should be allowed to refuse institution to an incum bent on the grounds of extreme youth or age, physical incapa city or insufficient testimonials. A priest thus refusec institution could appeal to the archbishop of the province o the provincial court. All transactions concerning the sale o livings should be conducted in public and duly registered, witl power to the parishioners to object to an appointment. The Act of 1828 which had legalized resignation bonds in favour o near relations (the notorious 'Warming-Pan Act') should be

for his failure to control a monster protest rally in Hyde Park. He was ar Ecclesiastical Commissioner and chairman of the Great Western Railway.

repealed. And a ban on the sale of next presentations was recommended by a majority of the commissioners.[27]

The report was published a year before Disraeli's fall from office. It had no immediate results, but the advent of a new Liberal government under Gladstone in 1880 prompted a fresh series of patronage Bills. All in turn fell by the wayside, though in one or two cases not without a struggle.

A Bill introduced in the Commons in 1881 by E.W. Stanhope reflected the thinking of the royal commissioners in seeking a ban on next presentations and the repeal of the 'Warming-Pan Act' of 1828. But it extended the possible grounds for refusing institution to an incumbent by adding mental incapacity and immoral conduct to youth, old age and physical infirmity. And it broke new ground by proposing the establishment in every diocese of a five-man diocesan patronage board consisting of the bishop and two members each of the clergy and laity. The new boards would be empowered to accept gifts or bequests of money for the purchase of advowsons, and to present to benefices where the patronage would otherwise have lapsed to the bishop.

Stanhope's Bill made little headway: in its author's view because it had been deliberately obstructed by a few Nonconformist MPs. It was reintroduced in a bowdlerized form later in the year, but again without success. Similar Bills in 1882 and 1884 fared no better. Nor did a number of more radical Bills which sought to restrict the sale of advowsons to certain classes of patron. The only Bill of this sort to survive its passage through Parliament during the 1880s was the Pluralities Act Amendment Bill, the brainchild of Bishop Temple. Its object was to make more efficient provision for the appointment of curates in parishes suffering from the negligence or incapacity of incumbents. It became law in 1885.

* * * * * * * * * *

A final word must be said here about the patronage of new

churches, a large number of which were built during the nineteenth century to cater for the spiritual needs of a rapidl growing urban population. Many of these churches wer funded out of government revenue, and a series of parliamen tary measures was passed between 1818 and 1856 to keep th operation under control. The first such measure, the Churc Building Act of 1818, was considered such a milestone that was described by the Prime Minister, Lord Liverpool, on i introduction in the House of Lords, as the 'most importan measure' he had ever submitted to their lordships' considera tion. Its keystone was the grant of £1 million of governmen money for the purpose of building at least 100 churches.*[28]

The patronage of these churches presented peculia problems, the chief of which was their precise status. In th past, if a church had been a 'chapel of ease' to its paris church, the right to nominate its minister had belonged to th incumbent of that church. This right was recognized in the firs Church Building Acts, which reaffirmed that, if a parish wa divided into 'districts', its incumbent should nominate th district ministers as if to chapels of ease. If, however, distinc 'parishes' were hived off from the original parish, then th patron of that parish should have the right to present to eac new parish. Before long it became necessary to encourage th public to subscribe towards the building of new churches; an a clause in an Act of 1827 allowed the commissioners t declare the right of nomination to belong to persons buildin and endowing such churches. A later Act of 1840 permitte subscribers to nominate a patron after applying to build church.

---

*Then, as now, governments were loth to throw public money around. Th commissioners appointed to administer the Act were instructed to provide 'proper accommodation for the largest number of persons at the leas expense' – in other words, to build as cheaply as possible. Hence thei churches tended to be 'functional' rather than ornate.

The right of subscribers to determine a new church's patronage opened the way to a development that was to become not wholly beneficial – the growth of trust patronage, or the acquirement of advowsons by minority doctrinal factions in the Church. At first such trusts were mainly Evangelical, as we saw earlier in the case of Charles Simeon. But, from the middle of the nineteenth century onwards, the Ritualists, or Anglo-Catholics, also began to acquire control of livings of their own.

In spite of the dangers of extremism at both ends of the ecclesiastical spectrum, some bishops made a practice of offering the patronage of new city churches to groups willing to build and endow them. By the 1870s both they and the Ecclesiastical Commissioners had come to regard such trust patronage as the norm in new urban parishes. It was not until the next century, however, when the new-born Church Assembly attempted its own reform of the patronage system, that the issue of party trusts, linked as they were to partisan policies, became a real matter of controversy.

10

Forward to 1898

The series of rebuffs to attempts at patronage reform in th
early 1880s came as a damper even to so ardent a reformer a
Bishop Magee. A new champion was needed to recommenc
the battle and bring it, hopefully, to a triumphant conclusion
That champion was now to hand in the person of the nev
Archbishop of Canterbury, Edward White Benson, who ha
succeeded Tait in 1883. Benson had been the first Headmaste
of Wellington and (after a short interval) the first Bishop o
Truro. His translation to Canterbury had been secured b
Gladstone only after a stiff tussle with Queen Victoria, wh
would have preferred the much older Browne of Winchester.

The Liberal Premier's choice was justified, in that Benso
proved an energetic and resourceful primate throughout hi
thirteen-year reign at Lambeth. Moreover, no other archbisho
in Victorian times identified himself so markedly and so consis
tently with efforts to persuade Parliament to agree to ecclesias
tical reforms. From 1886 until his death ten years later Benso
was constantly at work on measures for reform, either by wa
of preparation, in the Convocation of Canterbury, or in Parlia
ment itself.

The time seemed to him ripe for battle. On 12 Decembe
1885 a memorial promoted by Professor Westcott, the futur
Bishop of Durham, and signed by most of the leading residen
members of the Senate of Cambridge University was presente
to the archbishops and bishops of the Church of England. I
expressed the belief that the Church had long suffered seriou

148

injury by the postponement of necessary reforms and urged immediate action on, among other matters, patronage. It was the first and most influential of many other resolutions, memorials, petitions and letters addressed to Lambeth Palace. Benson responded to the critics and agreed to take up the challenge on their behalf.

For his first patronage Bill of 1886 he relied much on the wisdom and experience of Magee, who proved one of his closest collaborators in its framing and was able to boast to his friend MacDonnell: 'It was curious for me to find my seed sown eleven years ago "bearing fruit", clause after clause, in the forthcoming Bill, "after many days"'.[1] In its finished form the Bill sought to abolish the traffic in livings by making sales of advowsons invalid unless made to, or with the approval of, patronage boards to be set up in every diocese. These diocesan 'councils of public patronage' would have the power to purchase and hold advowsons, to receive money towards such purchases, to approve or disapprove proposed purchases of rights of patronage, and to exercise such rights of presentation as came to them from their advowsons. The boards were to be more wide-ranging in their powers than those envisaged by the Stanhope Bill of 1881, so it was hardly surprising when the new Bill was denounced by Lord Grimthorpe as the most revolutionary measure that had been brought forward since the Long Parliament. In fact it cut far too deeply into vested interests to have much chance of being passed; and the dissolution of Parliament which followed Gladstone's defeat on the second reading of his first Home Rule Bill ensured its early demise.

Nothing daunted, Benson came back the following year with a revised version of his Bill. This substituted for the councils of public patronage 'councils of presentation': these were to have similar powers to the former, but their members were to be chosen by a complicated system of clerical and lay election. In the event the new councils proved no more popular with the Lords than the old ones. The Prime Minister, Lord Salisbury, moved an amendment to delete them from the Bill on the ground that they introduced an objectionable elective principle into the management of church patronage. But the lay peers were not the only ones to object to the councils of presentations. These were apparently the result of a sudden brainwave on the part of the Archbishop, who had not consulted even so close a colleague as Magee before including them in the text of his Bill. Magee poured out his feelings in a letter to MacDonnell:

> The Archbishop has overloaded [the Bill] with a number of complicated and rather fantastic provisions for a great Diocesan Council of Presentations, none of which I ever saw or heard of until now, and has poorly stated his reasons for so doing. These damaged the Bill, and him and us, in the eyes of the Lords. I did not like to throw him over publicly and totally, but I did disparage the Council, and intimated that I cared little about it.[2]

Magee had every reason to feel aggrieved, as he had made a powerful speech two days earlier (during the debate on the second reading) which, in the opinion of at least one bishop, had 'saved the Bill'. In a letter to MacDonnell on the state of play Magee reported that things had indeed 'looked very black' at the start of the evening:

> No less than *six* peers came to tell me that they feared they must vote against the Bill, and one of them (Brabourne) was even prepared to speak against it! My first hour in the House was spent in lobbying these worthy aristocrats, and beseeching them to allow the second reading. Then I coached [the Bishop of] London [Temple] on the points on which they disliked the Bill, and warned him that, unless we showed ourselves quite open to alter or omit these, all was over with us. He took the hint and spoke very judiciously and dexterously, though a little heavily. He was followed by Lord Cowper as patron of seventeen livings, who spoke like a gentleman, but all in the old style about the right and innocence of selling benefices.[3]

150

Luckily one fervent opponent of the Bill who had denounced it at the start of the debate was not there to put in his oar a second time. Lord Grimthorpe was unavoidably absent. 'His effort on Monday', Magee told MacDonnell, brought on a fit of the gout, and thus I was not tempted to say sundry things that his presence might have provoked me into saying'.[4] In the event the Bill survived both its second and its third readings in the Lords; but, in spite of a promise to Benson by Salisbury that he would make it a government measure in the Commons, it somehow failed to make the passage to the Lower House. Perhaps, in the end, it was no bad thing. In its original form the Bill of 1887 was similar in all material respects to that of 1886. By the time, however, that it had run the gauntlet of Salisbury and his fellow advowson-holders in the Lords, it had been watered down into a form very different from the earlier Bill – though the Archbishop thought that it would still 'have done much to extirpate the worst evils connected with our advowson system and to leave the great undeniable benefits intact which flow from so much patronage being in the hands of the laity'. Nevertheless, the *Spectator* prophesied that, if it were passed, the Bill 'will be called the Archbishop's and will be Lord Salisbury's'.[5] It was to be another five years, and the Liberals again in power, before Benson returned to the fray.

He was emboldened to do so by the successful passage in 1892 of the Clergy Discipline Bill. This Bill had been carried in the House of Commons 'with *loud cheers*', he wrote at the time – 'and we have been everlastingly saying and hearing that no Church Bill could ever pass Parliament again'.[6] Patronage, however, was to prove a much harder nut to crack than discipline; and it took six more years' labour and half a dozen abortive attempts before the Benefices Act of 1898 finally reached the statute-book.

Benson summed up his dilemma thus in July 1892, when he took soundings for his Bill of the following year:

151

I find myself awkwardly placed in the matter of patronage ...
No one feels more strongly that the Trust of an Advowson
ought never to have acquired a money value and that the right
way of dealing with sales is to abolish them. This line is taken
by [the Bishop of] London and Herschell, who would do away
utterly with them after two more avoidances. But this 'after' is
a mere trick, I think, to make them now *seem* valueless when
the time comes, and on the other hand the Law has by abun-
dant and long continued action given a value and allowed it to
pass from hand to hand like other values. I feel how the future
will be unable to realise that decent people could have lived
under such a scheme. But I can't feel that as Archbishop it is
my place to confiscate and set an example of confiscation.[7]

Benson thought that the Commons would probably agree to
pass a Bill prohibiting sales of advowsons but would reject one
which, though improving the system by stamping out gross
abuses, would tend to perpetuate it. The Lords, by contrast
with a much greater number of advowson-owners, would
decline to pass a Bill seeking an outright ban on sales. His
problem was to devise a compromise measure which would
satisfy both Houses. His first attempt was framed on the lines
of his Bills of 1886 and 1887, but dispensed with the over-
elaborate 'councils of public patronage' and 'councils of
presentations'. It did attempt, however, to deal with priests
incapable of exercising an adequate ministry. It gave diocesan
bishops the power to compel the resignation of an incumbent if
any three parishioners issued a formal complaint that he had
been incapacitated from the due performance of his duties for
at least three years 'by continuing mental or bodily infirmity'.
In the event the Bill fared no better than its predecessors – and
on this occasion Benson found even his colleagues on the
episcopal bench unenthusiastic. On 16 March 1893, the day on
which he was to move the second reading of his Bill, nearly all
the bishops with seats in the Lords excused themselves from
attending. This drove Benson to fury. 'They are utterly
parochially minded', he complained, 'and Church Opening

and Confirmations ("important Diocesan engagements") are alleged as reasons for non-attendance at anything Imperial [e.g., Lords debates] ... To a Bishop of the younger sort the Diocese is much more than the Church'.[8]

The next attempt at reform was a Bill introduced into the Commons in 1894. Its principal features, like those of the Archbishop's Bill of the following year, were clauses aimed at sales of advowsons with 'vacant possession'. The Bill of 1894 provided that no right of presentation should be exercised within two years of the transfer of an advowson, and that its resale by an incumbent within two years of his institution should be prohibited. The Bill of course had Benson's backing and, like his Bill of 1893, represented not his own ideal solution so much as a 'careful collection of improvements which ... it would be indecent to refuse but which would make a considerable difference to our powers of dealing rightly with cases'.[9] Indecent or not, the Commons gave the Bill the thumbs-down; and the Archbishop's Bill of 1895, which reduced the two-year minimum period to a single year, fared no better. It was carried in the Lords, but the Dissolution of Parliament following the fall of Lord Rosebery's Liberal government made further progress hopeless. Like its two predecessors it had been an attempt not so much to reconstruct the patronage system as, in Benson's words, 'simply to quell *evasions* of the Law'.[10]

He refused to be deterred by his succession of rebuffs. In 1896, the last year of his life, he introduced yet another Bill into the House of Lords. His 'Benefices Bill' attempted to deal with two separate but linked subjects: patronage and clergy discipline. He took this course against his own better judgment, as the Bill had necessarily to be both long and complicated. It also lent itself to attack on two separate fronts: by so-called defenders of 'property' (i.e., advowsons) and by those who considered the Bill's measures to secure the resignation of ailing or negligent incumbents unnecessarily severe. In

the event, however, it passed its second reading by a large
majority and was not too severely mauled at the committee
stage. It was only when it came back to the Lords for its third
reading that the obstructive tactics of its opponents sealed it
fate. It could only have been successful with government
backing; but the Salisbury administration was unprepared to
devote the amount of time needed, so the Bill fell by the
wayside.

Benson had spent ten years in his unsuccessful attempts to
reform the patronage system. His repeated failures were due
partly to the strength of the opposition to any tampering with
rights of 'property', but also to defects in the Archbishop'
own temperament which made him not the ideal man to be
carrying reforms through the House of Lords. He was not a
born parliamentarian, being less effective in the Lords than on
the platform or in the pulpit. He was too compressed in his
speech-making, and never learned the trick of making the same
point over and over again. He was heard with respect, but not
always with comprehension. In the words of Chancellor Lewis
Dibdin, 'his notes contained only the heads of his speech, with
here and there a carefully packed sentence much too full of
ideas ... which he would read from his paper without the
emphasis of manner essential to make a listless audience
attend, and without allowance for their mental pace'.[11] Which
was a polite way of saying that many of the peers were too dim
to understand what Benson was driving at.

The Archbishop's greatest disappointment throughout these
years was, as he saw it, the lukewarmness of the Conservative
Party towards his efforts at reform. He may have underesti
mated the difficulties in the way of a government which
included among its members a number who were indifferent, if
not downright hostile, to the Church. But he could certainly
compare its leader, Lord Salisbury, unfavourably with his
Liberal rival, Mr Gladstone. Both were devout churchmen
but, whereas Gladstone had taken enormous pains to consult

154

Benson on Church matters, Salisbury as often as not ignored him. On one occasion Benson confided to his diary: 'Heard that X. is to be Bishop of Y.; as we have a Conservative Government and he is a High Churchman, neither he nor the Premier vouchsafe to communicate with me either before or after. (Never did.)'[12] On another occasion he complained: 'A Conservative Government believes the Church so sure to side with it that it takes no pains and exhibits no principles'.[13] And, in a moment of real indignation, he wrote: 'In eight or ten years there has been constant effort ... it is entirely owing to the Government that all effort fails'.[14] His real bitterness over Tory lukewarmness was revealed in a throwaway remark to a friend: 'The Radical party chastised the Church with whips, but the Conservatives with scorpions'.[15] The Liberal Gladstone, not the Conservative Salisbury, was the statesman to whom he could really unburden himself; and it was while attending Sunday-morning service with the Gladstones in Hawarden church that, on 10 October 1896, he died. The former premier commented: 'It was a soldier's death – a noble end to a noble life'.[16]

* * * * * * * * * *

Fortunately for the Church, Benson's successor in the primacy, Frederick Temple, was as zealous in the cause of patronage reform as had been Benson himself – and was as determined as his predecessor had been to endeavour to stamp out the worst abuses in the system. His first attempt was a Bill introduced into the Commons in 1897. It failed. Success, however, came the following year, when the Salisbury administration was at last persuaded – not least by the pressure of public opinion – to deal with the subject itself, instead of leaving it to bishops in the Lords and to private members in the Commons. The resultant government Bill – which became law as the Benefices Act of 1898 – was short and businesslike and struck effectively at the worst abuses of the patronage system. It rested on the concept that parishioners had rights as well as patrons, and that those rights were worthy of respect.

The Act abolished both resignation bonds and donatives (the latter were transmuted into ordinary livings). It made illegal the sale of next presentations. It required the sale of advowsons to be registered. It forebade their sale by auction unless sold in conjunction with a manor or with a neighbouring estate of at least 100 acres. It required a new declaration against simony much more stringent than the existing one. And it widened the powers of a bishop to refuse institution. He could now do so in case of an incumbent's physical, mental or moral unfitness, his inadequate professional experience, his grave pecuniary embarrassment, or his misconduct or neglect of his duty in an ecclesiastical office.

Laypeople hoping for a greater say in the choice of their pastors were admittedly disappointed. The Act required a bishop to give the churchwardens only one month's notice of his intention to admit a man to a benefice, and refrained from specifying any precise procedure for objecting to an appointment. However, all but the most fanatical critics of the existing system conceded that the Act represented a significant step forward. It put the clergy at long last on a par with those in comparable professions. In urging its acceptance Salisbury pointed out that private patronage in the Church was the last surviving example of a 'very extensive system when in all parts of the State large numbers of offices were purchasable for money'. The Prime Minister alleged, somewhat simplistically that reform had been held back by distrust of the episcopal office: the new proposals were a belated admission that an increase in the power of the bishops at the expense of the patrons might prove in fact to be in the best interests of the laity.[17]

Private patrons entered the twentieth century bloody to a certain extent, but basically unbowed. They were now restricted in the exercise of their rights and had to show greater

156

discretion in asserting them. But they were still in possession of their 'property', even though that 'property' was recognized more openly than in the past to have a spiritual dimension. The next stage in the reform of the system was not to come for another quarter of a century. It followed close on the heels of the Enabling Act of 1919, which gave the Church of England a substantial measure of self-government.

11

The Pace Quickens

The Enabling Act accelerated the pace of patronage reform. No longer was the Church required to go through the parliamentary hoops every time it wanted to modify any of its existing practices. Provided that Church opinion was satisfied that a particular reform was desirable, it was likely to be approved by the National Assembly of the Church of England (as the Church Assembly was called in its earlier days). Only in very rare instances, as in the case of the revised Prayer Book proposals of 1927–28, did Parliament decline to accept an Assembly measure. In the case of patronage reform the half-dozen or so measures which received the Assembly's final approval in the interwar years went through Parliament, if not on the nod, at least without a serious challenge.

Patronage reform was a concept which churchpeople of all schools of thought could support to a greater or lesser extent. It was one of the first issues to be tackled by the fledgling Assembly, which appointed a committee to examine the extent of the problem and to make recommendations for its solution. In its initial report the committee justly observed that to a large number of churchpeople the whole system of the sale of advowsons was morally intolerable. It pointed out that, of the 14,000 English benefices, about half were still vested in patrons who could legally sell their rights of patronage. As a first step towards ending this continued traffic in livings, the committee recommended a measure to amend the Benefices Act of 1898 - which itself had removed some of the worst abuses of the

158

patronage system. The chief improvements proposed by the new measure were that it forbade the sale of advowsons after the next two vacancies from the date of the passing of the measure (14 July 1924); and that it prohibited a clergyman from presenting himself to a benefice either directly or else indirectly through his wife or a trustee. To persuade patrons not to be tempted to sell their livings during the two-vacancies period of grace, a carrot was held out to them in the form of a financial grant for their livings from the Ecclesiastical Commissioners if they made a formal declaration that their advowsons were no longer capable of sale. (As will be seen, however, the carrot proved insufficient.) The Benefices Act (Amendment) Measure 1923 was approved by the Church Assembly and usefully extended the outreach of the 1898 Act.

The Assembly had now got the patronage bit between its teeth, but its next two attempts at reform came to grief. The aim of both abortive measures was to give parochial church councils (PCCs) a say in the appointment of their incumbents.

The Parochial Church Councils (Further Powers) Measure proposed that, when a patron had made his selection, the PCC would have the right to object to his nominee; and, on receipt of the objection, the bishop might refuse institution. The precise grounds of refusal were not, however, to be passed on to the incumbent-designate – who might therefore, critics pointed out, become a 'marked man' whose future reputation would be injured by a charge which he had never been allowed to hear. There was considerable opposition to the measure in the Church Assembly, though in the end it was passed – only to be rejected by the Ecclesiastical Committee of Parliament, on the ground that it contravened a basic principle of justice.

The Parochial Church Councils (Additional Powers) Measure fared worse, failing even to reach the Ecclesiastical Committee. It differed from its predecessor in two respects. First, when a PCC had told the bishop that it disapproved of the patron's nominee, it had to inform both the patron and the incumbent-designate, in writing, of the grounds for its objection; secondly, the bishop was then to be empowered not so much to refuse institution as, if he thought fit, to 'regard the presentation as having been withdrawn'. The new measure was an improvement on the previous one, in that it at least allowed a priest deemed unfit for a living to know the reason for his alleged unfitness; but, as it allowed him no right of reply to his critics, it was likewise open to strong objections. In a Church Assembly division by houses the measure was passed by the Laity by 159 votes to 26, but rejected by the Clergy by 103 votes to 95. There was a tie in the House of Bishops, with 15 votes going either way. Commenting on the 'unfortunate' division between clerical and lay opinion on the issue, the editor of *Crockford's Clerical Directory* tartly observed: 'It is conceivable that the working chairmen of Church Councils [i.e., the incumbents] are the better judges of the character and capacity of these bodies'.[1]

One likely consequence of the passing of the Benefices Act (Amendment) Measure of 1923 had been foreseen even before the measure reached the statute-book. This was that a great many livings might be thrown on the market while sales were still permitted – i.e., *before* two vacancies had arisen. In the words of the *Church Times*, 'it will be now or never to get rid of them'.[2] The paper's prophecy proved only too accurate. The next few years saw the sale of a considerable number of livings which had been unloaded by patrons while there was yet time. Most of these were eagerly snapped up by the various patronage trusts, which were ever on the lookout for opportunities to extend their empires and so (hopefully) perpetuate their own brands of churchmanship in the parishes thus acquired. The trusts were mostly at opposite ends of the ecclesiastical spectrum. Two of them, the Society for the Maintenance of the Faith and the Guild of All Souls, represented Anglo-Catholic interests; but the great majority were controlled by Evangelical bodies such as the Church Pastoral

Aid Society and the Martyrs' Memorial and Church of England Trust.

This last-ditch bid by the trusts to buy advowsons while the going was still good was condemned by moderate churchmen, but went on nonetheless. It was soon reaching alarming proportions. The *Church Reform League Chronicle* for December 1925 referred to advertisements in the *Times* and the 'Protestant Press' offering advowsons for sale and enlarging on the comfort of the vicarages, the size of the vicarage gardens and the social amenities of the neighbourhood – just as if they were back in the bad old days of the nineteenth century. Four years later the *Church Times* carried an article by a Sussex incumbent deploring the 'wholesale manner' in which wealthy Protestant trusts were buying advowsons. The article pointed out that four of these recently-acquired livings had a Tractarian tradition which was now put at risk: 'The unfortunate parishioners will be compelled to accept arbitrary changes, with incumbents pledged not even to permit a vase of flowers, to say nothing of a crucifix, on the Holy Table'. In an editorial comment in the same issue the paper deplored such 'blatant mobilization of money-bags to stem the Catholic revival' – and glibly pointed out that the two small Catholic trusts, which together owned less than one-eighth of the advowsons in the hands of the Protestant trusts, never purchased the right of presentation to a living with any idea except of preserving that which was already established.*[3]

Anglo-Catholics were not the only ones to deplore the activities of the Protestant trusts. So doughty an Establishment figure as Bishop Hensley Henson of Durham published a

---

* Privately-appointed incumbents sometimes felt less inhibited. As recently as the 1980s an extreme Anglo-Catholic priest was appointed by a local landowner to a benefice in the diocese of Rochester previously served by a moderate Evangelical. Within weeks of his arrival he had introduced a liturgical set-up completely opposed to that of his predecessor – and, in the process, had managed to offend a considerable number of his parishioners.

polemical pamphlet in 1932, *Sibbes and Simeon*, drawing attention to the extent of the damage that was being done. He urged the legal abolition of the trusts, on the ground that they operated as an independent power within the Church of England and buttressed the 'unnatural rigidity of partisan churchmanship'. Though nominally concerned with trusts of every party, the pamphlet was clearly aimed at the Evangelicals. This was apparent from the two characters named in its title: Sibbes was a prominent seventeenth-century Puritan who had helped to organize the purchase of tithes; Simeon was the nineteenth-century 'saint' of Evangelicalism who had founded the best known of the Protestant patronage trusts. It was no surprise to Henson that his pamphlet should be condemned by Evangelicals and applauded by Anglo-Catholics. In spite of his strictures, however, the trusts continued to buy up advowsons as opportunities arose – though, in the case of newly-created parishes, the Church Assembly clipped their wings in 1943 by vesting the patronage of such parishes in the hands of the diocesan bishop.

But that is to anticipate. The early 1930s saw the passing into law of a number of Church Assembly measures which shifted the balance of power from patrons to parishioners.

The first of these, the Benefices (Transfer of Rights of Patronage) Measure, 1930, had as its object the placing of some sort of check on the secret transfer of advowsons. It obliged a patron wishing to transfer an advowson by sale or otherwise to disclose his intention both to the bishop of the diocese and to the PCC of the parish concerned. A PCC had fourteen days in which to inform the bishop of any objections it had to the proposed transfer, and the bishop had then to notify the patron of these objections and, if necessary, to confer with the PCC regarding the transfer. The measure made no mention of what would happen if an impasse was reached at the conference between the bishop and the PCC. Presumably it was hoped that the patron could be persuaded to have second thoughts about the desirability of the transfer.

Immediately after the Church Assembly had given its final approval to the measure, it passed to a much more dramatic piece of business: nothing less than a measure to abolish without compensation the sale of all advowsons. The new measure was introduced by Sir Thomas Inskip (later the first Viscount Caldecote), a doughty Protestant who had been a leading adversary of Prayer Book revision in the Commons debates of 1927–28. The Assembly found itself closely divided on the issue. The votes in the Houses of Bishops and Clergy were exactly equal (nine to nine and ninety-three to ninety-three). But the House of Laity declined to give general approval to the measure by ninety-eight votes to eighty-two, so it fell to the ground. The opposition centred on the absence of any form of compensation to the holders of what were still regarded as items of property possessing a certain market value. Property, in the eyes of many members of the Assembly, was sacred. To abolish advowsons without a penny of compensation seemed to them a high-handed proceeding – or, in the words of the editor of *Crockford's Clerical Directory*, an 'almost catastrophic moral blunder'.[4] No doubt Parliament would have felt the same if the measure had been agreed by the Assembly and passed on to it for its approval.

The next significant move in the process of reform came a year later with the passing of the Benefices (Exercise of Rights of Presentation) Measure 1931. This at last gave parishioners a formal voice in the appointment of their incumbent, even if only in the negative sense of being able (through their church-wardens) to protest against a nominee of whom they disapproved. Likewise bishops were granted a discretionary power to refuse any really unsuitable nominee.

The nuts and bolts of the measure were clear enough. On a vacancy or impending vacancy in a parish, the PCC was empowered to make representations to the patron as to the conditions, needs and traditions of the parish – but without mentioning the name of any particular clergyman. The patron – and this was the nub of the matter – could not then exercise his right of presentation without either the consent of the churchwardens (acting as the representatives of the PCC) or, if such consent was not forthcoming, the bishop's approval. A body of advisers was to be set up in every diocese which might be consulted by the bishop before giving or withholding his approval, and which had to be consulted if so required by the patron and the PCC.

The measure was held by its framers neither to place an undue restriction on the patron's right of presentation nor to injure the reputation of a clergyman whose suitability was questioned. But its effectiveness depended to some extent on the canniness of the churchwardens, who had to be not only zealous and strong-minded but well informed about the necessary legal hoops through which they had to pass. In theory the bishop could overrule the churchwardens, but the hope was that he would refrain from doing so without an overwhelmingly good reason. By and large the measure secured some sort of safeguard against the imposition of, say, an extreme Evangelical incumbent on a parish with a long Anglo-Catholic tradition. The measure did not apply to benefices in the patronage of the Crown, but these represented only about 8 per cent of the total number.

The next milestone, a comparatively minor one, was the Benefices (Diocesan Boards of Patronage) Measure 1932, which provided for the establishment of a board of patronage in every diocese. The boards had the power to acquire and exercise rights of patronage, taking over any advowsons which had previously been vested in the diocesan boards of finance. Each patronage board was to consist of the diocesan bishop as chairman; three priests and five laypeople elected by their respective chambers of the diocesan conference; and the archdeacon and rural dean in whose archdeaconry and deanery a benefice under discussion was situated. When a benefice in the patronage of a diocesan board was vacant, or when the board was acting as arbitrator between patron and parish, representatives of the parish were to be allowed to attend the board meetings and have their say. They could not be present, however, when names were under discussion, nor record a vote when a decision was to be reached. The effective disfranchisement of those who would be most directly affected by a diocesan-board appointment was a blow to radical critics of the system, but was justified by the system's defenders on the principle that a man should not be a judge in his own cause.

The final pre-war measure was also a significant one, in that it gave PCCs the right, in certain cases, to acquire by compulsory purchase the patronage of their own benefices – or, in the words of the *Church Times*, 'to re-purchase ... the advowsons which have been surreptitiously bought up with Protestant gold since 1924'.[5] The main object of the Benefices (Purchase of Rights of Patronage) Measure 1933 was to circumvent the party trusts which had been busy buying up advowsons ever since the date on which the Benefices Act (Amendment) Measure had come into effect: 14 July 1924. The new measure provided that, when an advowson had been sold since that date, the PCC might require the purchaser to sell it back to them at a price to be determined by arbitration. It would then be vested in the diocesan board of patronage. The right of presentation was thus not bequeathed to the PCC itself. But a parish of one ecclesiastical colour would be likely to find the board much more sympathetic to its tradition than a partisan trust of an opposite colour. The effectiveness of the measure (which likewise did not apply to benefices in the patronage of the Crown) depended in the long run on how many of the 300 or so parishes concerned would be able and willing to dip into their pockets to produce the necessary cash. A sizeable number in fact did so.

Final approval for the measure was obtained in the Church

Assembly only after a division by houses. The Bishops approved it by 13 votes to 5, the Clergy by 111 votes to 38 and the Laity by 109 votes to 51. The considerable opposition showed that the issue was not as clear-cut as it appeared to its supporters. The latter might regard it as a triumph for elementary justice, but to some critics it appeared unjust to deprive party trusts of assets which had been legally acquired. The *Church Times* spoke for the majority, however, when it declared: 'The power of the Protestant money-bags has now been effectively checked'.[6]

12

Paul and After

The Benefices Measure of 1933 was the last in the series of reforms of the patronage system approved by the Church Assembly in the period before the Second World War. It was not until fifteen years after the end of that war that the Assembly again took the reforming bit between its teeth. In previous generations the path to each wave of reform had been prepared by such cumbersome devices as royal commissions, select committees and the like. Now the Assembly put its faith in the efforts of a single individual: Leslie Paul (1905–85), a distinguished Anglican author, philosopher and sociologist who had recently been director of studies at Brasted Place Pre-Theological College in Kent.* Following a Church Assembly motion in July 1960 he was appointed to enquire into the deployment and payment of the clergy – and to make recommendations.

The famous (or notorious) Paul Report appeared in January 1964. Its proposals were unashamedly radical. It recommended the abolition of the parson's freehold, the ending of the distinction between beneficed and unbeneficed clergy, and the introduction of a new form of parochial unit, the 'major parish', for heavily populated towns and extensive areas of countryside. Moreover, it took the bull by the horns and said that patronage should go. Leslie Paul proposed the establishment

---

* It was Paul, not John Osborne, who was the originator of the phrase 'Angry Young Man': the title of an autobiography he published in 1951.

of a Clergy Staff Board to transform patronage into a more open and systematic appointments advisory system, and of regional boards which would act as local agents in the process of transformation. He minced no words in his denunciation of the existing system. The machinery of deployment and preferment, he said, was very simple to describe: 'it does not exist'.[1]

Paul conceded that patrons did their best, often under great difficulty, to find the men they wanted, but he deplored the fact that PCCs enjoyed no real power in the matter. They had the right to be consulted, and even to object to a nominee, but had no recourse to the material information on which a proper objection could be based; nor could they suggest candidates of their own. The present chaotic system, in Paul's judgment, 'often makes for an unseemly scramble for names and hasty presentation of untested curates to livings. It also makes for the neglect of older, quieter, unspectacular parish priests'.[2]

Radicals in the Church of England get nowhere in a hurry. If their proposals are to be made palatable to traditionalists, they have to be watered down – often to such an extent as to be almost unrecognizable. Such was the fate of the Paul Report.

On its appearance it was at once denounced by traditionalist opinion. The proposed transformation of the patronage system was described by a writer in the *Church Times* as 'destructive of the spirituality of the Church of England'; while, in an editorial in the same issue, the paper declared that it was not a priest's vocation to be 'a pawn on a vast, impersonal, bureaucratic chessboard'.[3] A year after the report's publication the Church Assembly referred most of its major proposals for consideration by a commission chaired by Canon Fenton Morley, vicar of Leeds. The commission reported in June 1967 – and confirmed that it shared Leslie Paul's views on the shortcomings of the present method of appointing and deploying the clergy. It proposed that, in every diocese, patronage would be taken over by a diocesan ministry commission (an adaptation of Paul's regional boards); appointments policy in the

Church at large would be coordinated by a Central Ministry Commission (Paul's Clergy Staff Board). The freehold would be replaced by a limited leasehold tenure of office.

The Morley Report fared no better than the Paul Report. The opposition in the Church Assembly was led by the Bishop of Chester, Gerald Ellison (later Bishop of London), who published a pamphlet upholding the merits of the present freehold and patronage system and disparaging its proposed replacement.* When the Assembly debated the report a deep division of opinion was at once apparent. Although many members favoured a moderate reform of the patronage system, the Morley proposals for its complete abolition went too far for the Assembly as a whole.

After chewing them over for three years it again postponed a decision by asking for yet another committee to consider the more contentious Morley suggestions. The Terms of Ministry Committee (TMC) began its deliberations in the spring of 1971 under the chairmanship of Bishop Rodger of Manchester and produced its first report in June 1972.

By then the Church Assembly had been replaced by the General Synod, the keystone of the new system of synodical government which, in the autumn of 1970, had replaced the original system set up under the Enabling Act. It had been the hope of would-be reformers that the new system would open up the Church to a brave new world of radical renewal. Their hopes were to be disappointed. The new system was in effect the old system under a different name. Although about 40 per cent of the members of the first General Synod had never belonged to the Church Assembly, the mixture as a whole was

---

* Bishop Ellison (of whom Bishop George Reindorp once remarked that 'like most oarsmen he believes that he can only move forward by looking backward') in fact changed his mind on this issue. In a General Synod debate in 1975 he remarked that he had 'no great attachment' to the system of private patronage.

169

much the same as before. The membership was analysed in *The Christian Century* as roughly 10 per cent Anglo-Catholic, 25 per cent Evangelical, 25 per cent Radical/Reformist and 40 per cent a 'mixture of Everything and Nothing'. 'From such a body', the paper observed, 'it would be reasonable to expect a modicum of reform but obviously nothing resembling a revolution'.[4] The forecast proved only too accurate. From the start the proceedings of the Synod were dominated by the old Church Assembly hands. In the words of a radical historian, Trevor Beeson:

> The General Synod is not a new body: it is the old Church Assembly reconstituted and renamed. The style and atmosphere of the Synod is indistinguishable from its predecessor. Those who entered with the intention of shaking the Church of England to its foundations have now discovered that the machinery of ecclesiastical government is not easily moved and that the Synod is able to absorb and neutralize the most savage assaults upon the *status quo*.[5]

Not surprisingly, the first report of the new TMC succeeded in watering down the Morley recommendations on patronage. Morley's proposed diocesan ministry commissions found no favour. Instead, the TMC proposed the setting up of parish appointment committees when particular vacancies arose. Each committee would consist of the bishop of the diocese, the patron and representatives of the parish concerned, thereby securing the representation of diocese, patron and parish in 'even balance'. In true Anglican vein, the committees would seek to secure agreement on the nomination of new incumbents by consensus rather than by majority vote.

This modest reform, however, proved, surprisingly, too modest for a majority of the Synod's members to swallow. While welcoming the report's other suggestions (such as a compulsory retirement age of 70 for the clergy, the setting up of a Central Stipends Authority, and the creation of the post of adviser on clerical appointments to the archbishops), the Synod agreed (by 209 votes to 177) to refer back to the TMC its proposals for the reform of the patronage system, with a request that they should be reconsidered in the light of the manpower situation in the Church at large.

The TMC obliged and, a year later, came up with a report devoted entirely to the reform of the patronage system. It made the right radical noises. It declared that the system was an outdated concept which should be replaced by 'something akin to partnership'. It proposed that patrons should be retained, but that the parish and diocese should be brought in as equal partners in the appointment process. It then repeated the call made in its previous report for parish appointment committees on which bishop, parish and patron could all cooperate when a new incumbent had to be nominated. But it linked this proposal (as requested) to an overall deployment policy. It recommended that, within the diocese, the deployment of available manpower should be seen as part of the responsibility of the diocesan pastoral committee, and that the bishop should establish, from within its membership, a panel to act for the diocese in staffing matters. Two members of the TMC stuck their necks out with a 'memorandum of dissent', recommending that patronage should be completely abolished. In the event they came within a whisker of getting their way.

The session of the General Synod at which the new proposals were discussed (5 July 1973) was in fact the occasion for a moment of high drama. One of the two committee dissentients, T.F. Hunt, in an amendment to the main motion, asked the Synod's standing committee 'to bring forward proposals for the abolition of patronage and for a new system of making appointments to benefices whereby both the needs and views of the individual parish, and the deployment and other needs of the Church in the diocese and more widely, are given due weight'. This open throwing of the radical hat into the ring produced first an impassioned debate (Hunt's supporters included the Archbishop of Canterbury, Michael Ramsey) and then a close division. In the House of Clergy there were ninety five votes in favour of the Hunt amendment to sixty-seven against; in the House of Laity there were seventy-five votes in favour to sixty-six against; in the House of Bishops there was a dead heat, with fourteen votes cast on either side.

The chairman, R.R. Feilden, rose in an attempt to call for a recount in the House of Bishops, but was challenged by an expert on procedural matters, Oswald Clark. There could be no recount, Clark insisted. A tie, under the Synod's standing orders, was tantamount to a negative vote; so the amendment having been lost in one house, automatically fell to the ground There were one or two half-hearted attempts to contest this view, but Clark stuck to his guns and his point was upheld. So at the end of the day, victory rested with the traditionalists. If only one of the many bishops absent from the count had been present to vote for the amendment, the Synod would have signalled the ending of the patronage system (though that would have been to reckon without Parliament). The radicals owed their defeat to the call for a vote by houses – a political device favoured by hardened Synod hands as a convenient means of playing for a draw or slowing down a movement for reform, since a motion need be defeated in only one house to be automatically lost. A straight majority vote would have secured the radicals' objective. As it was, they were now back to square one, the Synod having rejected not only the Hunt amendment but also the original proposals in the report.

* * * * * * * * * *

There was now a pause of eighteen months as each side licked its wounds and an eight-member working party under the chairmanship of Prebendary Henry Cooper drew up a fresh set of proposals for the reform of the patronage system. Its report, published in January 1975, introduced a new factor into the equation, in the hope of satisfying both traditionalists and radicals. It envisaged two co-existing alternative methods of appointing incumbents, one retaining the patronage element in a modified form, the other dispensing with it altogether. 'Alternative A' went beyond the existing requirement for consultation between patron and parish by making the offer of a benefice dependent on the concurrence of the PCC as well as of the bishop. 'Alternative B' replaced the patron by a three-person selection committee consisting of the bishop or his nominee and of two persons chosen by the PCC.

The Cooper Report was intended simply as a 'basis for discussion'. In the event, and perhaps surprisingly, the Synod, when it debated the report on 7 February 1975, came down decisively in favour of the proposals by 228 votes to 51, an overall majority of 177. But the wheels of the Church of England grind exceedingly slow; and it was to be another three years before the proposals took legislative shape in the form of the Patronage (Benefices) Measure. The measure incorporated as its main plank the two Cooper alternatives, leaving the decision as to which alternative to adopt to each individual parish. If, however, a parish opted for Alternative B, its decision would be irreversible and the patron's rights would be extinguished for ever. The framers of the measure prudently exempted from its provisions all parishes in the patronage of the Crown.

So far, so good. The measure received general approval in all three houses of the Synod when it was debated in July 1978. But then the inevitable traditionalist reactions set in, and it was amended in various minor ways before being referred to the forty-three diocesan synods in July 1980. The synods were asked to vote on a motion approving the underlying principle of the measure: that there should be two alternative methods of appointing incumbents to benefices. The result, however, was a typical Anglican stalemate: twenty synods voted in favour of the motion and twenty-three against it. A report to the General Synod by its standing committee warned that, if it decided to go ahead with a measure retaining the two alternative methods of appointment, it would do so in the knowledge that the proposals did not have sufficient support in the Church at large.

In the background was the spectre of an incensed House of Commons eager to champion the traditionalist laity. MPs, it was predicted, would be indignant if the General Synod failed to change course in response to the voting figures in the dioceses. The simple answer, in the opinion of the standing committee, was to draw the measure's radical teeth by referring it to a fresh revision committee with instructions 'to remove in their entirety the provisions previously made for the "presentation-by-selectors" system'. This was indeed to emasculate the measure beyond recognition – though the standing committee attempted to disguise its butchery by making soothing noises about a revised measure 'designed to achieve a thorough system of modernization and reform'.

In the event the Synod tamely accepted the notion that 'nanny knows best' and, on 11 February 1983, sent the measure back for the necessary surgery. So, with the *coup de grâce* delivered to the proposed dual system of appointment, the existing system of patronage was set to continue. Two years later, on 12 February 1985, the measure was accorded final approval by the General Synod (the overall vote in favour was 270 to 4). It had proved awkward to the end; and more than forty 'special amendments' had been needed to tidy it up at its final drafting stage (they all went through the Synod almost on the nod). The result may well have been, in the words of Bishop Yates of Gloucester, summing up the debate, a 'sensible piece of reform, bringing up-to-date a mass of untidy legislation'. But the Synod could not pretend that what had come in with a bang in 1978 had gone out in 1986 with anything more than a whimper.

Even now there was a further period of delay. First the measure had to pass through the parliamentary hoops. This i

id successfully in the summer of 1986, being approved by the
Commons in June and by the Lords in July. But then there
was another procedural hurdle to surmount. One of the
measure's innovations was the requirement to compile a full
register of patrons in all the forty-three dioceses of the Church
of England. Work on this began in October 1987 and took
fteen months to complete. So it was not until 1 January 1989
that the measure came into full effect.

Apart from the register, what changes did it actually introduce? Basically, only two of any significance. First, a patron
was required to obtain the agreement of the churchwardens of
vacant parish (or two other laypeople nominated by the
PCC) as well as the agreement of the bishop for his nominee.
An increasing number of patrons were already conceding the
PCC's right of veto, so the measure was to that extent
legalizing existing practice. Secondly, although the measure
llowed anyone to be a patron, only a communicant member
of the Church of England or of a Church in communion with
could actually present a priest to a bishop for institution. So,
here patrons failed to qualify on this count, they had to
ominate someone else to act on their behalf.

The Patronage (Benefices) Measure 1986 may be described
s the baby of the patronage proposals contained in the Paul
Report. That report had been published on 16 January 1964.
The new measure came into effect on 1 January 1989. It was a
ery small baby to have emerged after a gestation of almost
xactly twenty-five years, but its birth was typical of the way in
which the Church of England operates.

Paul had begat the Morley Commission, which had begat
Bishop Rodger's TMC. The TMC in its turn had given way to
he Cooper Working Party, whose proposals for two alterna-
ve systems of appointment formed the controversial core of
he Patronage (Benefices) Measure in its original form. The
ting (and the main point) of that measure was removed after a
harp division of opinion among the diocesan synods had

175

raised an amber light and the prospect of a *nolle prosequi* on the part of Parliament. So, in the event, the comparativ mountain of a measure that had emerged in the bright dawn o 1978 was transformed into the mouse of its final reincarnation in 1986.

The appearance of defeat for the radical cause was, howevei to some extent illusory. This was because of a significant nev development that was overtaking the Church in the 1980s: th gradual nibbling away at the parson's freehold by the device o appointing men to be priests-in-charge rather than incumbent of benefices. The ostensible reason for this move was an acut shortage of priests, especially in the countryside, which mad the amalgamation of parishes in groups of two, three or mor a desirable economy measure. But, so long as the freehol existed, the formation of a grouped ministry depended on th consent of the incumbents involved – and one dissentien rector or vicar could hold up a scheme indefinitely, or at leas until his freehold tenure was ended by his departure throug death or resignation. The device adopted to minimize delays o this sort was to suspend the presentation of parishes needed to form parts of groups. This was legally possible under th Pastoral Measure of 1968. It meant that a bishop woul appoint a man as priest-in-charge of a parish for a limite number of years, so that he would not be in a position to hol up a desired amalgamation indefinitely.

The net result of the increasing number of parish merger also meant that the patrons of the constituent parishes of new united benefice would have to agree among themselves a to the man or (after 1993) woman they wished to see appointe as their parish priest. And, as the diocesan bishop would, a likely as not, be himself the patron of at least one of thos constituent parishes, he would be in a good position to exer pressure on his fellow-patrons to choose the candidate h wanted. Plenty of examples have occurred within the las twenty years of bishops manipulating private patrons in thi

176

way to suit their own convenience or that of their dioceses rather than the interests of the parishes concerned. A few of these will be mentioned in my next chapter, when I take stock of the patronage position in the Church of England today. The net result, however, is that private patrons have rather less say and diocesan bishops a great deal more say in the appointment of parish priests than they did a generation ago. It is all part of that process of 'gradualism' by which the Church contrives to introduce reforms into its system of government one step at a time.

13

Compromise Solution

The Church of England is notoriously a Church where compromise is king. Nowhere was this better demonstrated than in the long-running debate on parish patronage in the second half of the twentieth century. The heady dreams of the radical prophets of the 1960s gradually faded away as the traditionalists and pragmatists battled back. And the succession of hard-fought debates in the General Synod ensured that though lip-service was paid to the need for reforming the system, reform when it came was extremely modest.

Patronage today is exercised under the terms of the Patronage (Benefices) Measure, 1986. Its most important proviso is to allow a PCC, through a formal power of veto, a real say in the process of selecting its incumbent. That process is akin to the present process of selecting diocesan bishops in the Church of England. The Prime Minister is handed a couple of names by the Crown Appointments Commission (CAC) but has the right to reject both names if he or she sees fit.*

In the case of a PCC there are obvious hazards in being too choosey. An episcopal patron may not be too concerned if his first or even his second nominee is turned down by the PCC representatives; but he would soon become irritated if candi

---

* This right was not known to have been exercised until 1997. It was in that year that the new Labour Premier, Tony Blair, declined to present either of the CAC's two nominees for the see of Liverpool to the Queen for her approval, but told it to think again.

178

late after candidate was rejected. In some cases pressure is brought to bear on an independent-minded PCC, and its representatives are told in so many words to accept the next episcopal nominee or risk being denied a new incumbent indefinitely. The danger is that, in the face of this sort of pressure, a PCC may bow the knee and, as a result, find itself saddled with an unsuitable incumbent.

In one case known to me the PCC representatives turned down the first candidate on the ground that a man who had ministered only in inner-city areas would be unsuited to a rural benefice – but then, in the face of archdiaconal rumblings, went on to accept a nominee who was heavily involved, as a county councillor, in local politics. The thought of possible conflicts of loyalties arising between pastoral and political interests was already alarming many in the benefice when the problem resolved itself by the candidate's withdrawing for personal reasons only a few weeks before his institution. A new candidate was hastily found by the authorities, was accepted by the PCC representatives and proved a great success.[1]

The general provisions of the 1986 Measure are, as befits an Established Church, highly elaborate and hedged around with provisos and safeguards of various sorts. When a vacancy occurs in a parish the PCC is required to prepare a statement (often known as a 'parish profile') describing the conditions, needs and traditions of the parish. This is for the guidance both of the patron and of the diocesan bishop (assuming they are not the same). The PCC may ask the patron to advertise the vacancy in the regular lists circulated by the Clergy Appointments Adviser and perhaps also in the two Anglican weeklies, the *Church Times* and the *Church of England Newspaper*. But the patron is not obliged to do so, and by no means every vacancy is advertised.

When a patron has decided on a suitable candidate to offer to a parish he has first to obtain the approval of the bishop and the PCC representatives – those 'representatives' being a

179

small number of members (they usually include the churchwar
dens) appointed by the PCC for that specific purpose. It is the
who 'vet' on behalf of the full council each candidate presente
by the patron. Where either the bishop or the PCC representa
tives regard a candidate as unsuitable, the presenting patro
must be notified in writing of the grounds on which the objec
tion is made. The patron can only offer a benefice to a pries
when he or she has been formally approved by the bishop an
the representatives. If the first candidate is rejected for an
reason, then a second candidate is presented – and so or
Although the 1986 Measure is intended to involve parishe
most closely in the appointment process, that involvement i
essentially negative rather than positive. A PCC, through it
representatives, can veto the patron's candidate, but it canno
suggest one of its own. The key man in the process is th
bishop. If he is not the actual patron himself, he will often b
consulted by the patron over possible candidates when
vacancy arises, and is therefore frequently in a position t
influence the result.

Bishops almost always get their way. A case brought to m
attention concerned a benefice in a Midlands diocese in th
patronage of the diocesan. When the rector retired four poten
tial successors were entertained to lunch separately by the PCC
representatives, and each spent a day touring the benefice. Th
representatives were enthusiastic about one of the four, but, o
naming their preference to the local area bishop, wer
informed that the parish could not have him (no reason given)
They could either accept another of the candidates or start th
process all over again. As one of the churchwardens was o
the brink of a nervous breakdown, the representatives did a
they were told and plumped for their number-two choice. H
began well enough, but then announced his intention of drasti
cally reordering the church. My informant commented to me
'I suspect that he had been instructed to do this from highe
up, and that is why his candidature was supported by th

ishops'. The dispatch of the other three candidates was presumably a piece of window-dressing.[2]

The exact interpretation of the Patronage Measure and the practices pursued under it vary from diocese to diocese, but the general guidelines are clear enough. The code of practice for the Measure states: 'Representatives should be PCC members who are in a position to become actively involved in the process of selecting the incumbent and to reflect the views of the PCC in doing so, and in approving or refusing to approve an offer of the benefice to the priest selected by the patron'.

Many benefices are still in the gift of patronage trusts, which are usually on the alert against undue influence being exercised by the diocesan bishop. The Church Pastoral Aid Society (CPAS), for instance, supports local churches in resisting the 'more damaging consequences' of the Church of England's current financial crisis by (a) challenging moves to suspend presentation to benefices whenever the local church's pastoral and evangelistic ministry would be weakened; (b) where the patron's and PCC's rights *have* been suspended, pressing for suitable priest-in-charge appointments; (c) questioning a diocese's preference for an appointment from within rather than from outside the diocese; (d) monitoring systems for pastoral reorganization and seeking to amend them if 'unsuitable' mergers are proposed.[3] The CPAS has over 500 benefices within its gift – second only to the Lord Chancellor and rather more than all the other Evangelical trusts combined. Its incumbents are required to be 'gospel-orientated and pledged to mission', a stipulation that is often reflected in the society's advertisements published in the Church press. A typical one, seeking a vicar for a parish in the 'conservative evangelical tradition', stipulated that he (*sic*) 'will trust Jesus Christ as the only Saviour, and accept the authority of Scripture as the inspired word of God; will preach with authority, and base his teaching on Holy Scripture; will have a commitment to church growth through evangelism; will respect our pattern and style

of services . . .; will not be a charismatic'.[4] The CPAS's twelv
trustees meet regularly to pool their expertise in creating short
lists and monitoring progress towards filling vacancies.

A number of patronage societies of 'orthodox Anglica
persuasion' are linked informally in a body known as th
Private Patrons' Consultative Group (PPCG). They include, o
the Catholic wing, the Church Union, the Society for th
Maintenance of the Faith and the Guild of All Souls and, o
the Protestant wing, the Church Society. Like the CPAS, th
PPCG is concerned at the constant suspending of presentatio
permitted under the Pastoral Measure of 1983; this allow
freehold rectors and vicars to be replaced by priests-in-charg
enjoying only a limited tenure of office. Another concern of th
PPCG is when several parishes of differing traditions c
churchmanship are brought together in a single benefice unde
an incumbent who may be much more sympathetic to on
tradition than to another.

Suspension of presentation is usually proposed in the intei
ests of pastoral efficiency. In practice it is a useful device fc
preventing a freehold incumbent from holding up a merger c
benefices indefinitely – in spite of the stipulation in the code c
practice for the Measure that 'care should be taken to alla
any fears on the part of the clergy, patrons and parishione
that suspension of presentation is being used either to exclud
the right of patrons, or to frustrate the "parson's freehold"
The PPCG, in a set of guidelines for patrons, points out tha
before a priest-in-charge is appointed in place of an incumben
the bishop is required to consult the PCCs and, 'so far as
practicable', the patron. The PPCG comments: 'It is difficult t
imagine circumstances in which it is not possible to consult
patron. Nevertheless there are those bishops still who presei
the patron with a *fait accompli* and make no effort to consul
This should be made the subject of formal complaint when
occurs'.[5]

One area of uncertainty in the revised patronage systei

ncerns the grounds on which a nominee can be turned down
a bishop or PCC. The Measure gives no clear indication on
e matter. The code of practice attached to it suggests that
ossible grounds for refusing consent could be failure on the
art of the candidate to meet some vital requirement in the
arish profile, or a personality defect which would be likely to
event him or her from exercising an effective ministry in the
arish. The Measure has not been in operation long enough
r this grey area to be delineated in sharper colours. And, so
r, little use has been made of the procedure allowing an
opeal to the archbishop of the province.

One such case where an appeal *was* made concerned the
arital status of the incumbent-designate. On that occasion
)ecember 1994) the Archbishop of Canterbury ruled that it
as inappropriate to identify such status as a necessary condi-
on of appointment. This verdict could well establish a prece-
ent for the future, and put paid to any PCC hope of
otaining a priest of 40 with a pretty wife and two children
ther than the better-qualified celibate offered it by the
atron. Far more contentious grounds for refusal would be if
e nominee was known or suspected to be a practising
omosexual, or if his views on the ordination of women did
ot square with those of the PCC.

The right of presentation to a parish, though it can no
nger be bought and sold, can still be transferred by deed of
ft. Such an abdication of responsibility on the part of a
atron should, in the opinion of bodies like the PPCG, be
sisted. A diocesan bishop, the PPCG points out, is always
ateful for the opportunity to add to his patronage and so
rward a centralizing tendency in his diocese. Against this
ust be set the value of an independent parochial voice. To
ansfer the patronage of a benefice from private to diocesan
nds should be a last resort, 'all other possibilities having
en explored and found wanting'.[6] There are two ways of
oking at the matter of course. The bishop can be regarded as

a benevolent uncle seeking to bring order into the muddle of mixed system of official and private patronage. Or he can t regarded as a Big Brother attempting to include more an more parishes within his own patronage empire.

In a few exceptional cases the transfer of patronage doe however, seem inevitable. A parish in East Anglia was in tl gift of the local landowner, a peer. In 1988, shortly before new rector was due to be instituted, the patron who ha appointed him was sent to prison on a drugs-related charg The rector was presented to the bishop by the peer's hal brother acting on his behalf. When the living next fell vacaı the patron, still in the grip of his addiction, failed to act ı time, so the patronage passed to the bishop of the diocese who, following the popular fashion, appointed a priest-iı charge to fill the vacancy.[7]

A comparatively recent arrival on the patronage scene is tl Clergy Appointments Adviser. This official, who dates froı 1977, is appointed by the Archbishops of Canterbury an York both to assist priests to find suitable new appointmen and to assist patrons and others responsible for makir appointments to track down suitable candidates.

The Adviser in the early 1990s was Canon Ian Hardake whose ideas about his job can be found in the pages of tw contemporary accounts of the Church of England whic appeared within a few weeks of each other in 1993. Each yeɛ Hardaker interviewed between 400 and 500 clergymen seekir a job and sent them a fortnightly list of vacancies. He to Michael De-la-Noy, one of the two authors, that his role wɛ to assist bishops and patrons in head-hunting and that, thouɡ patronage was entirely illogical, it led to healthy variety – 'ʋ would not find it easy to devise a system of appointments thɛ would serve us better'.[8] To Ysenda Maxtone Graham he put slightly differently: the system of job-finding was a mess, 'but think there's a certain beauty in the mess'. He told her that ł per cent of livings were then still in the gift of private patron

ıd in one recent case, she discovered, echoes of the nineteenth
ɛntury were still around. The would-be incumbent was rung
ɔ by a landowning friend of his family's and asked whether
ɛ wanted a living in the country – 'You're not against blood
ɔorts, are you?'[9]

Hardaker found that the parishes hardest to fill were the
ɛally remote rural ones and those on large and often vanda-
ɛed housing estates. The most user-friendly were country-
ɪwn parishes with a single church in the centre of the town
ıd a recognizable community.[10] Hardaker hunted his heads
ɔm an office behind Church House, Westminster, from which
ɛ issued forth to attend bishops' staff meetings and post-
ɪdination conferences.

Six per cent of Church of England livings are still in the gift
ˈ the Crown – and, as such, remain outside the scope of the
ɪtronage Measure of 1986. The majority of Crown livings are
  fact administered by the Lord Chancellor, and most of the
  mainder by the Prime Minster as lineal descendant of the
ɔrd High Steward. The division was finalized by Henry VIII
  1536, the Lord Chancellor being empowered to handle all
ɪings worth £20 a year or less and the Lord High Steward
ɔse above that figure. (This was an updating of Edward III's
ɔ-mark limit.) Both Premier and Lord Chancellor employ
ɪpointments secretaries to administer their respective
ıtronage empires; and over the years a succession of such
ˈficials have exercised their stewardship with a conscientious
ill.

An insight into the workings of the Lord Chancellor's
ɛpartment in the early 1960s was obtained by Paul Ferris
ɦile researching for a book on the Church of England. The
  clesiastical secretary at that time was a certain Brigadier
ɛrnard Watkins, an ex-army officer who carried out his duties
ı War Office principles. 'I have to know everything about a
ɑn before I put him in a parish', he told Ferris, 'and I get
ɪnfidential reports – testimonials aren't worth the paper

185

they're written on'.[11] Attached to one of the walls of Watkins office in Dean's Yard, Westminster, was a large map wi coloured pins showing his master's livings – especially thic down the eastern side of England. He maintained an elabora filing system and told Ferris: 'When a man comes into o orbit he gets a personal file, and this isn't destroyed till the da he dies'.[12]

Another file listed all the parishes in the Chancellor's gi with notes about size and type of population (such as 'agricu tural' or 'shopkeepers'), the current incumbent's age ar stipend, and details of the churchmanship (e.g., 'Central-plu and parsonage house. The importance of the parish (Watkins's eyes, that is) was indicated by a code showir whether it was rated 'top-notch' with a tradition to keep u ordinary urban or ordinary rural. The object of the exerci was to fit the parish to the incumbent.

The personal file was packed with details of priests wantir to move. Coloured discs eased the assessment process. Re indicated a man already in one of the Chancellor's living dark-blue a 'market-town type', light-blue a potential cano green someone suggested by an MP ('If that happens the ma must have a reason for doing it').[13]

Watkins paid a personal visit to each of his parishes at lea once every five years, with the aim of getting to know both t parishes and the priests who filled them. 'I want to prove you', he told Ferris,

> 'that Crown patronage is as well administered as any and a sight better than most. We're appointing leaders in the country-side ... and fundamentally there's no difference between leaders of the Church, leaders in the Services or leaders in industry ... You can't expect the earth, because we're short of supply. But I'm an old soldier, and, having wandered round the world for thirty-two years, I've got some idea of selecting leaders'.[14]

Watkins was running the Lord Chancellor's parishes

generation ago. But there is no reason to suppose that his successors have proved less efficient in their duties – though they have no doubt replaced card-indexes with computers.

* * * * * * * * * *

Patronage scandals in the eighteenth-century image may have died out, but even in the closing years of the twentieth century the whiff of politics in the selection of a parish priest could occasionally be scented. A case which caused no small stir in 1983 concerned the parish of Leiston-cum-Sizewell in Suffolk. Leiston itself is an unassuming market town, but Sizewell is dominated by a nuclear power-station; and it was Sizewell's nuclear connection that caused the controversy.

A vacancy had arisen in the benefice, the patron of which is a City of London livery company. And the guidelines issued by the company (and apparently drafted by the local archdeacon) suggested that the new incumbent should *not* be an anti-nuclear campaigner, since such a stance could (in the patron's view) seriously impede his pastoral work. The archdeacon was even quoted as saying: 'You can't have a man who is vicar of the parish walking up and down with a placard'.[15] This sort of remark caused indignation both locally and farther afield. It is hard to believe that a conscientious priest, however passionate his personal political views, would allow them to influence his pastoral care of his parish.

It is dangerous to be too dogmatic about patronage today, as hard cases can always be found – and quoted. Take Oxbridge colleges, for instance. Some ensure that one of their chaplains or fellows keeps in touch with the incumbents of parishes within their gift. Others fail to do so, and rarely show up except on formal occasions. At the institution of one incumbent, a bishop complained, the college had not even bothered to send its porter to present its candidate. The same bishop revealed that, in most cases, any concern shown was limited to little more than coming into the picture when a vacancy arose.

187

'As one vicar commented, "I simply had a letter saying that, i
ever I was in X, they would be glad to see me"'.[16] Such .
casual attitude is in marked contrast to the far greater interes
shown by the Lord Chancellor's ecclesiastical secretary in hi
employer's livings.

It is the same with patronage trusts. Some take infinite car
over their appointments and courteously assume that th
bishop of the diocese, backed by the added pastoral knowledg
of his staff, will have opinions about the pastoral needs of th
parish and the choice of the incumbent to whom he is to b
father-in-God. They consider these opinions to be at least a
worthy of consideration as those of the parish representatives
But not all the patronage trusts are as accommodating to th
powers-that-be. Some care more for preserving a party lin
than anything else – though perhaps not quite so dogmaticall
nowadays as a generation ago. The literature they produce
such as guidelines for parishes seeking an incumbent, ma
seem harmless enough; but of course that is no guarantee tha
what goes on at interviews behind closed doors is invariabl
free from any partisan element.

Evangelical parishes are now so thick on the ground tha
Evangelical trusts have insufficient livings within their gift t
accommodate all the faithful in search of a benefice. So man
priests of Low Church persuasion must seek other patrons
and perhaps find themselves in parishes less Evangelical tha
they would wish. Then, if they wish to tone down the church
manship of their parish, they must do so at a sensibly cautiou
pace if they wish to avoid offending those holding differen
views from their own – and perhaps emptying the church as .
result.

Anyway, in these days of constantly shifting church goal
posts, it is unwise to be too dogmatic in case one is overtake
by events. To take a single example, in the old days stric
Evangelicals took the 'north-end' position at the altar (or 'hol
table', as they would style it) when celebrating Holy Commu

nion, whereas Anglo-Catholics or middle-of-the-road Anglicans would take the east-end position, facing away from the congregation. Nowadays more and more priests of all traditions of churchmanship adopt the west-end position, facing the people, so the preferred point of the compass is no longer a cast-iron indicator of a priest's churchmanship.

* * * * * * * * * *

An increasing number of parishes nowadays are united in various ways and require the exercise of joint patronage by their respective patrons. Under the 1986 Measure the individual patrons are required to reach agreement on the choice of a candidate for a united benefice. In the event of their failing to agree, no offer of presentation can be made – it is not permitted to decide the issue by majority vote. In many such cases one or more of the uniting parishes is in the gift of the bishop; and he may be expected to influence his co-patron or patrons in supporting the candidate of his own choice. Indeed many private patrons are only too relieved to accept the bishop's nominee and be spared the chore of tracking down a suitable candidate of their own.

Such 'manipulation' by the bishop has its uses. A suburban Anglo-Catholic parish in Kent well known to me is, through a quirk of history, in the gift of the ultra-Evangelical rector of the nearby market town. Up until the 1960s each vacancy in the living was a period of much perturbation for the PCC, anxious lest a priest more of the rector's way of thinking than of the congregation's be appointed. In 1967, however, the parish was merged with its next-door neighbour, which was in the gift of the bishop, to form a united benefice. As a result the PCC is now less fraught when a vacancy occurs, since the bishop would never allow the rector to dictate the choice of a new incumbent and risk upsetting the congregation with a priest of his own way of Protestant thinking.

Of course, as long as the present mixed system of patronage persists, horror stories are likely to abound. But a vacancy can be looked at in two ways: as an opportunity for a parish to be offered the best available successor to the outgoing incumbent, and as an opportunity for a bishop, on behalf of his diocese, to make better use (in his judgement) of limited resources by merging it with its neighbour. The parishioners of course much prefer to have their own parish priest living on the spot; the diocesan powers-that-be are anxious to use their financial resources as wisely as possible. Each side is arguably justified in its attitude: it is simply a case of reaching an acceptable compromise with the least possible friction. The growth of the local non-stipendiary ministry in recent years has eased the position in a number of dioceses. Such local priests may not live in the local parsonage, but at least they are at hand to administer pastoral care when the need arises.

* * * * * * * * * *

Few nowadays would wish to go back to the unreformed patronage system as it existed in the Church of England a century or more ago. The present situation may still be far from perfect, but at least it represents a good Anglican compromise. Private patrons are still around in sizeable numbers, and most of them carry out their limited responsibilities with commendable care and diligence. Their teeth have to a large extent been drawn, in that they can no longer impose their candidates on parishes unwilling to accept them. But at least they are still there and, in view of the innate conservatism of the Church of England, are likely to remain so for the foreseeable future. The radical reform of the patronage system advocated in the Paul and Morley reports in the end got nowhere in the face of that conservatism; and it seems unlikely that any fresh attempt to resume the debate will be made. The number of private patrons may well dwindle away in the

190

course of time, and the importance of their role decrease still further as more and more parishes are merged or find their presentation suspended. But, if the substance is gone, at least the shadow will remain.

SOURCE REFERENCES

1 Friends in High Places

1. G.B. Shaw, *Captain Brassbound's Conversion*, Act iii.
2. Charles Gore (ed.), *Essays in Aid of the Reform of the Church*, pp. 198–202.
3. *ibid.*, p. 204.
4. *ibid.*
5. R.S.T. Haslehurst, 'Victoriana', pp. 71–2.
6. Gore, p. 205.
7. *ibid.*
8. D.R. Hirschberg, 'The Government and Church Patronage in England, 1660–1760', pp. 111ff.
9. M.J.D. Roberts, 'Private Patronage and the Church of England, 1800–1900', p. 202.

2 God and Caesar

1. S.C. Carpenter, *Eighteenth-Century Church and People*, p. 111.
2. *ibid.*
3. R.B. Martin, *Enter Rumour*, p. 141.
4. D.R. Hirschberg, 'The Government and Church Patronage in England, 1660–1760', p. 130.
5. Albert Hartshorne (ed.), *Memoirs of a Royal Chaplain, 1729–1763*, p. 5.
6. Norman Sykes, *Church and State in England in the Eighteenth Century*, p. 152.
7. *ibid.*, p. 153.
8. Norman Sykes, 'The Duke of Newcastle as Ecclesiastical Minister', p. 61.

9. C.J. Abbey and J.H. Overton, *The English Church in the Eighteenth Century*, p. 25.

10. A.T. Thomson (ed.), *Memoirs of Viscountess Sundon*, vol. i, p. 421.

11. *ibid.*, vol. ii, p. 153.

12. Martin, p. 143.

13. S.W. Baskerville, 'The Political Behaviour of the Cheshire Clergy, 1705–1752', p. 76.

14. Stebelton H. Nulle, *Thomas Pelham-Holles, Duke of Newcastle: His Early Political Career*, p. 46.

15. Sykes, 'The Duke of Newcastle', p. 64.

16. Carpenter, p. 110.

17. Thomas Newton, *The Life of Dr Thomas Newton*, pp. 101–2.

18. *ibid.*, p. 100.

19. Hirschberg, p. 128.

20. Reed Browning, *The Duke of Newcastle*, p. 186.

21. Norman Sykes, *Edmund Gibson*, pp. 109–10.

22. John, Lord Campbell, *The Lives of the Lord Chancellors*, vol. v, p. 166.

23. *ibid.*, p. 635.

24. George Crabbe, jnr., *The Life of George Crabbe*, p. 117.

25. *ibid.*, p. 131.

26. Alan S. Bell, *Sydney Smith*, p. 73.

3 Caring for One's Own

1. Anthony Trollope, *Clergymen of the Church of England*, pp. 29–30.

2. Francis Warre Cornish, *A History of the English Church in the Nineteenth Century*, p. 328.

3. Albert Hartshorne (ed.), *Memoirs of a Royal Chaplain, 1729–1763*, p. 266.

4. (John Wade), *The Extraordinary Black Book*, pp. 22–3.

5. William Purcell, *Onward Christian Soldier*, p. 89.

6. Norman Sykes, *Church and State in England in the Eighteenth Century*, p. 158.

7. *ibid.*, pp. 161–2.

8. D.R. Hirschberg, 'The Government and Church Patronage in England, 1660–1760', p. 136.
9. Sykes, p. 213.
10. Margaret Shaw, *Laurence Sterne*, p. 35.
11. *ibid.*, pp. 69–70.
12. James Boswell, *Life of Samuel Johnson*, vol. i, p. 320.
13. *ibid.*, vol. ii, p. 151.
14. *ibid.*, vol. i, p. 476.
15. Irene Collins, *Jane Austen and the Clergy*, p. 27.
16. Giles Hunt, 'A Real-life "Jane Austen Clergyman"', pp. 151–7.
17. Mary Clive (ed.), *Caroline Clive*, p. 28.
18. *Hansard's Parliamentary Debates*, 3rd Series, vol. 224, col. 1453.
19. *ibid.*, vol. 260, col. 976.
20. *Church Times*, 27 March 1874.
21. *ibid.*, 25 August 1876.
22. *ibid.*, 20 September 1872.
23. Thomas Gisborne, *An Enquiry into the Duties of Men . . .*, pp. 32–3.
24. Sykes, p. 205.
25. Alan S. Bell, *Sydney Smith* p. 166.
26. M.J.D. Roberts, 'Private Patronage and the Church of England, 1800–1900', p. 204.
27. Charles Linnell, *Some East Anglian Clergy*, pp. 115–29.
28. Edward Carpenter, *Archbishop Fisher*, pp. 3–4.
29. *Hansard*, 3rd series, vol. 260, cols. 185–6.
30. Purcell, pp. 120–3.

4 Souls for Sale

1. *Hansard's Parliamentary Debates*, 3rd Series, vol. 260, col. 195.
2. Owen Chadwick, *The Victorian Church*, Part ii, p. 213.
3. Charles Gore (ed.), *Essays in Aid of the Reform of the Church*, p. 223.
4. *Hansard*, 3rd series, vol. 218, col. 906.
5. Charles Smyth, *Simeon and Church Order*, p. 246.
6. *ibid.*, p. 247.
7. Sabine Baring-Gould, *The Church Revival*, pp. 118–9.
8. Herbert Armstrong, *A Norfolk Diary*, p. 260.
9. *ibid.*, p. 268.

10. Diana McClatchey, *Oxfordshire Clergy, 1777–1869*, p. 5.
11. John Cannon, *Aristocratic Century*, pp. 63–4.
12. *ibid.*, p. 65.
13. Esme Wingfield-Stratford, *This Was a Man*, p. 133.
14. *ibid.*, p. 147.
15. *Hansard*, 3rd Series, vol. 260, cols. 184–5.
16. *ibid.*, col. 189.
17. *ibid.*
18. *ibid.*, cols. 190–1.
19. *ibid.*, cols. 191–2.
20. *ibid.*, col. 194.
21. *The Chronicle of Convocation* (of Canterbury), 8th V.R., vol. iv, pp. 21–3.
22. Peter Virgin, *The Church in an Age of Negligence*, p. 186.
23. *Hansard*, 3rd Series, vol. 224, col. 1222.
24. Alan S. Bell, *Sydney Smith*, p. 143.
25. Deirdre Le Faye (ed.), *Reminiscences of Caroline Austen*, pp. 18–19.
26. W.M. Palmer, *William Cole of Milton*, p. 8.
27. R.W. Ketton-Cremer, *Country Neighbourhood*, pp. 210–11, 219.
28. *Hansard*, 3rd Series, vol. 260, col. 195.
29. G.F.A. Best, *Temporal Pillars*, p. 59.
30. M.J.D. Roberts, 'Private Patronage and the Church of England, 1800–1900', pp. 214–5.
31. *Hansard*, 3rd Series, vol. 224, col. 1226.
32. Norman Sykes, *Church and State in England in the Eighteenth Century*, p. 189.
33. Arthur H. Cash, *Laurence Sterne: The Early and Middle Years*, p. 137.
34. Bell, p. 144.
35. John, Lord Campbell, *The Lives of the Lord Chancellors*, vol. v, p. 636.
36. (Josiah Bateman), 'Senex', *Clerical Reminiscences*, pp. 96–7.

5   Earning a Living

1. C.L.S. Linnell (ed.), *The Diaries of Thomas Wilson, D.D.*, 19 December 1731.

2. *ibid.*, 18 September 1732.
3. *ibid.*, 24 October 1733.
4. *ibid.*, 23 November 1733.
5. *ibid.*, 1 December 1733.
6. *ibid.*, 10 December 1733.
7. *ibid.*, 24 December 1733.
8. *ibid.*, 27 September 1734.
9. *ibid.*, 22 May 1735.
10. *ibid.*, 26 May 1735.
11. *ibid.*, 23 July 1735.
12. *ibid.*, 4 November 1735.
13. *ibid.*, 7 November 1735.
14. *ibid.*, 13 December 1735.
15. *ibid.*, 15 December 1735.
16. *ibid.*, 16 December 1735.
17. *ibid.*, 10 January 1735/6.
18. *ibid.*, 5 February 1735/6.
19. *ibid.*, 1 July 1736.
20. *ibid.*, 3 July 1736.
21. *ibid.*, 10 August 1736.
22. *ibid.*, 1 September 1736.
23. *ibid.*, 10 September 1736.
24. *ibid.*, 19 October 1736.
25. *ibid.*, 30 October 1736.
26. *ibid.*, 1 November 1736.
27. *ibid.*, 5 November 1736.
28. *ibid.*, 19 December 1736.
29. *ibid.*, 27 January 1736/7.
30. *ibid.*, 23 April 1737.
31. *ibid.*, 25 April 1737.
32. *ibid.*, 10 May 1737.
33. *ibid.*, 21 May 1737.
34. *ibid.*, 27 May 1737.
35. *ibid.*, 2 June 1737.
36. *ibid.*, 4 June 1737.
37. *ibid.*, 31 (*sic*) November 1737.
38. *ibid.*, 1 December 1737.

9. Georgina Galbraith (ed.), *The Journal of the Rev. William Bagshaw Stevens*, 30 November 1792.
0. *ibid.*, 13 November 1793.
1. *ibid.*, 18 November 1793.
2. *ibid.*, 22 November 1793.
3. *ibid.*, 13 December 1793.
4. *ibid.*, 29 January 1794.
5. *ibid.*, 2 May 1794.
6. *ibid.*, 19 June 1794.
7. *ibid.*, 30 June 1794.
8. *ibid.*, 30 December 1794.
9. *ibid.*, 31 December 1794.
0. *ibid.*, 3 January 1795.
1. *ibid.*, 8 January 1795.
2. *ibid.*, 31 January 1795.
3. *ibid.*, 20 February 1795.
4. *ibid.*, 22 February 1795.
5. *ibid.*, 27 February 1795.
6. *ibid.*, 28 February 1795.
7. *ibid.*, 1 March 1795.
8. *ibid.*, 16 April 1795.
9. *ibid.*, 12 April 1795.
0. *ibid.*, 24 May 1795.
1. *ibid.*, 8 August 1795.
2. *ibid.*, 12 November 1795.
3. *ibid.*, 24 February 1796.
4. *ibid.*
5. *ibid.*, 8 June 1796.
6. *ibid.*, 22 January 1797.
7. *ibid.*, 10 March 1797.
8. *ibid.*, 1 June 1798.
9. *ibid.*, 12 August 1798.
0. *ibid.*, 25 October 1798.
1. *ibid.*, 27 October 1798.
2. *ibid.*, 28 October 1798.
3. *ibid.*, 21 November 1798.
4. *ibid.*, 15 December 1798.

75. *ibid.*, 17 December 1798.
76. *ibid.*, 11 January 1799.
77. *ibid.*, 6 February 1799.
78. *ibid.*
79. *ibid.*, 20 March 1799.
80. *ibid.*, 15 April 1799.
81. *ibid.*, 24 April 1799.

6   The Parson and the Squire

1. *Hansard's Parliamentary Debates*, 3rd Series, vol. 218, col. 915.
2. Michael Hinton, *The Anglican Parochial Clergy*, p. 149.
3. Sabine Baring-Gould, *The Church Revival*, p. 136.
4. G.F.A. Best, *Temporal Pillars*, p. 51.
5. Hinton, p. 150.
6. R.W. Ketton-Cremer, *Country Neighbourhood*, p. 47.
7. James Obelkevich, *Religion and Rural Society*, pp.38–9.
8. *ibid.*, p. 38.
9. L.G. Mitchell (ed.), *The Purefoy Letters*, pp. 18–20.
10. Ketton-Cremer, *passim.*
11. John Beresford (ed.), *The Diary of a Country Parson*, vol. i, p 235.
12. *ibid.*, p. 294.
13. *ibid.*, p. 295.
14. C.D. Linnell (ed.), *The Diary of Benjamin Rogers*, p. 46.
15. *ibid.*, p. 50.
16. *ibid.*, p. 55.
17. Georgina Battiscombe, *John Keble*, pp. 39–40.
18. *ibid.*, pp. 173–4.
19. Margaret Shaw, *Laurence Sterne*, p. 36.
20. *ibid.*, pp. 70–1.
21. Brenda Colloms, *Charles Kingsley*, pp. 72–3.
22. Obelkevich, p. 39.
23. Gavin Hannah (ed.), *The Deserted Village*, p. xvii.
24. *ibid.*, p. xviii.
25. *ibid.*, p. xix.
26. *ibid.*, p. 110.

27. *ibid.*, p. iv.
28. Howard & Peter Coombs (eds), *Journal of a Somerset Rector*, p. 33.
29. *ibid.*, p. 34.
30. *ibid.*, p. 99.
31. *ibid.*, pp. 99–100.
32. *ibid.*, p. 100.
33. William Plomer (ed.), *Kilvert's Diary*, vol. ii, p. 239.
34. *ibid.*, vol. iii, p. 97.
35. *ibid.*, p. 100.
36. *ibid.*, pp. 102–3.
37. *ibid.*, p. 109.
38. *ibid.*, p. 114.
39. *ibid.*, p. 111.
40. Owen Chadwick, *A Victorian Miniature*, p. 89.
41. *ibid.*, p. 93.
42. *ibid.*, pp. 177–8.
43. William Purcell, *Onward Christian Soldier*, p. 89.
44. *ibid.*, p. 134.

7 Safety in Numbers

1. John Gascoigne, *Cambridge in the Age of Enlightenment*, p. 13.
2. L.S. Sutherland & L.G. Mitchell (eds), *The History of the University of Oxford*, vol. v, p. 115.
3. Gascoigne, p. 14.
4. *ibid.*, p. 102.
5. Sutherland & Mitchell, p. 116.
6. *ibid.*
7. Diana McClatchey, *Oxfordshire Clergy, 1777–1869*, p. 9.
8. Margaret Evans (ed.), *Letters of Richard Radcliffe and John James*, pp. 38–40.
9. John Beresford (ed.), *The Diary of a Country Parson*, vol. i, pp. 142–3.
10. Louise Creighton, *Life and Letters of Mandell Creighton*, vol. i, pp. 139–43.
11. McClatchey, p. 6.

12. Peter Virgin, *The Church in an Age of Negligence*, p. 183.
13. D.A. Winstanley, *The University of Cambridge in the Eighteenth Century*, pp. 323–6.
14. Thomas Gisborne, *An Inquiry into the Duties of Men...*, pp. 24–5.
15. Virgin, p. 218.
16. W.M. Jacob, *Lay People and Religion in the Early Eighteenth Century*, pp. 29–30.
17. David Verey (ed.), *The Diary of a Cotswold Parson*, p. 45.
18. *ibid.*, p. 150.
19. R.J. Wood, *Leeds Church Patronage in the Eighteenth Century*, p. 103.
20. *ibid.*, pp. 103–4.
21. *ibid.*, pp. 104–13.
22. C.J. Stranks, *Dean Hook*, pp. 44–7.
23. John Lock & T.W. Dixon, *A Man of Sorrow*, pp. 182–201.
24. *Hansard's Parliamentary Debates*, 3rd Series, vol. 218, col. 913.
25. Thomas Arnold, *The Principles of Church Reform*, p. 126.
26. *Hansard*, 3rd Series, vol. 224, cols. 1213–4.
27. *ibid.*, vol. 218, col. 912.
28. Charles Gore (ed.), *Essays in Aid of the Reform of the Church*, p. 228.
29. *Hansard*, 3rd Series, vol. 224, col. 1214.
30. *ibid.*, cols. 1213–4.
31. *ibid.*, cols. 1210–1.

8   Absentee Shepherds

1. C.J. Abbey & J.H. Overton, *The English Church in the Eighteenth Century*, p. 10.
2. *ibid.*, p. 14.
3. *ibid.*, p. 10.
4. C.K. Francis Brown, *A History of the English Clergy, 1800–1900*, p. 28.
5. *ibid.*, pp. 29–30; Norman Sykes, *Church and State in England in the Eighteenth Century*, pp. 147–8.
6. *Hansard's Parliamentary History*, vol. 36, col. 486.

7. Norman Sykes, *Edmund Gibson*, pp. 228–30.
8. S.L. Ollard and P.C. Walker (eds), *Archbishop Herring's Visitation Returns, 1743*, vol. i, p. xiv.
9. Arthur H. Cash, *Laurence Sterne: The Early and Middle Years*, pp. 138–9.
10. Sabine Baring-Gould, *The Vicar of Morwenstow*, p. 180.
11. (John Wade), *The Extraordinary Black Book*, p. 31.
12. Sykes, *Church and State*, p. 216.
13. H.A. Lloyd Jukes (ed.), *Articles of Enquiry Addressed to the Clergy of the Diocese of Oxford at the Primary Visitation of Dr Thomas Secker, 1738*, p. 42.
14. *ibid.*, p. 98.
15. *ibid.*, p. 76.
16. *ibid.*, p. 154.
17. *ibid.*, p. 99.
18. *ibid.*, p. 105.
19. *ibid.*, p. 131.
20. *ibid.*, p. 158.
21. *ibid.*, pp. 82–3.
22. *ibid.*, p. 152.
23. Ollard & Walker, vol. i, p. 21.
24. *ibid.*, p. 183.
25. *ibid.* p. 191.
26. *ibid.*, vol. ii, p. 158.
27. *ibid.*, p. 123.
28. *ibid.*, vol. i, p. 145.
29. *ibid.*, vol. iv, p. 131.
30. *ibid.*, vol. i, p. 218.
31. *ibid.*, vol. ii, p. 124.
32. *ibid.*, vol. i, p. 144.
33. *ibid.*, p. 66.
34. *ibid.*, p. xiii.
35. Thomas Gisborne, *An Enquiry into the Duties of Men...*, pp. 97–8.
36. Sykes, *Church and State*, p. 220.
37. *ibid.*, pp. 217–8.
38. G.C.B. Davies, *Henry Phillpotts*, p. 156.
39. Peter Virgin, *The Church in an Age of Negligence*, pp. 207–8.

40. Brown, p. 39.
41. *ibid.*
42. Brenda Colloms, *Charles Kingsley*, pp. 69, 72.
43. *Hansard's Parliamentary History*, vol. 36, cols. 469–70.
44. *Hansard's Parliamentary Debates*, 3rd Series, vol. 21, cols. 560–9, 631–4.
45. *ibid.*, vol. 23, cols. 860–7.
46. Virgin, pp. 192–3.
47. W.M. Jacob, *Lay People and Religion in the Early Eighteenth Century*, p. 22.
48. Virgin, p. 200.
49. Sykes, *Church and State*, p. 217.
50. (Wade), pp. 30–2.
51. *ibid.*, p. 35.

9 One Step at a Time

1. Peter Virgin, *The Church in an Age of Negligence*, pp. 196–7.
2. *Hansard's Parliamentary History*, vol. 36, col. 486.
3. *ibid.*, col. 884.
4. G.F.A. Best, *Temporal Pillars*, p. 59.
5. *Hansard's Parliamentary Debates*, 3rd Series, vol. 11, col. 1167.
6. *ibid.*, vol. 42, col. 926.
7. C.K. Francis Brown, *A History of the English Clergy, 1800–1900*, pp. 72–3.
8. Virgin, p. 211.
9. Brown, pp. 75–6.
10. M.J.D. Roberts, 'Private Patronage and the Church of England, 1800–1900', p. 214.
11. Bernard Palmer, *High and Mitred*, p. 82.
12. J.C. MacDonnell, *The Life and Correspondence of William Connor Magee*, vol. ii, p. 35.
13. *ibid.*, p. 3.
14. *ibid.*
15. *ibid.*, p. 4.
16. *ibid.*, p. 15.
17. *ibid.*, p. 16.

18. *ibid.*, p. 18.
19. *ibid.*, p. 19.
20. *ibid.*, pp. 21–2.
21. *ibid.*, p. 22.
22. *ibid.*, p. 32.
23. Roberts, p. 217.
24. MacDonnell, p. 33.
25. *ibid.*, pp. 36–7.
26. *ibid.*, p. 37.
27. Francis Warre Cornish, *A History of the English Church in the Nineteenth Century*, vol. ii, p. 333.
28. M.H. Port, *Six Hundred New Churches*, pp. 22–4.

10 Forward to 1898

1. J.C. MacDonnell, *The Life and Correspondence of William Connor Magee*, vol. ii, p. 219.
2. *ibid.*, p. 241.
3. *ibid.*, p. 240.
4. *ibid.*, p. 241.
5. A.C. Benson, *The Life of Edward White Benson*, vol. ii, pp. 74–5.
6. *ibid.*, p. 92.
7. *ibid.*
8. *ibid.*, p. 521.
9. *ibid.*, p. 560.
10. *ibid.*, p. 639.
11. *ibid.*, p. 99.
12. *ibid.*, p. 100.
13. *ibid.*
14. *ibid.*, p. 102.
15. *ibid.*
16. David Williams, *Genesis and Exodus*, p. 107.
17. M.J.D. Roberts, 'Private Patronage and the Church of England, 1800–1900', p. 222.

11 The Pace Quickens

1. (Crockford Prefaces), *The Editor Looks Back*, p. 27.

2. *Church Times*, 10 November 1922.
3. *ibid.*, 16 August 1929.
4. (Crockford Prefaces), p. 109.
5. *Church Times*, 24 March 1933.
6. *ibid.*

12 Paul and After

1. Leslie Paul, *The Deployment and Payment of the Clergy*, p. 107.
2. *ibid.*, p. 108.
3. *Church Times*, 17 January 1964.
4. *Christian Century*, 4 November 1970.
5. Trevor Beeson, *The Church of England in Crisis*, p. 131.

13 Compromise Solution

1. Private information given to the author.
2. *ibid.*
3. CPAS leaflet, *CPAS & Patronage*, April 1996.
4. CPAS leaflet, *Advertising a Vacancy*, October 1997.
5. PPCG booklet, *Exercising Patronage in the Church of England*, 1995, p. 10.
6. *ibid.*, pp. 1–2.
7. Private information given to the author.
8. Michael De-la-Noy, *The Church of England: A Portrait*, pp. 135–6.
9. Ysenda Maxtone Graham, *The Church Hesitant*, p. 55.
10. De-la-Noy, pp. 136–7.
11. Paul Ferris, *The Church of England*, p. 44.
12. *ibid.*, p. 45.
13. *ibid.*, p. 46.
14. *ibid.*
15. Article by Douglas Brown in *Church Times*, 11 February 1983.
16. Article by George Reindorp in *Church Times*, 23 August 1974.

BIBLIOGRAPHY

Place of publication is London unless otherwise stated.

Abbey, Charles J., with Overton John H., *The English Church in the Eighteenth Century.* Two volumes. Longmans, Green 1878.

Armstrong, Herbert B.J. (ed.), *A Norfolk Diary: Passages from the Diary of the Rev. Benjamin John Armstrong, M.A.(Cantab.), Vicar of East Dereham, 1850–88.* George G. Harrap 1949.

Armstrong, Herbert B.J. (ed.), *Armstrong's Norfolk Diary: Further Passages from the Diary of the Reverend Benjamin John Armstrong (1817–90).* Hodder & Stoughton 1963.

Arnold, Ralph, *The Whiston Matter: The Reverend Robert Whiston versus the Dean and Chapter of Rochester.* Rupert Hart-Davis 1961.

Arnold, Thomas, *The Principles of Church Reform.* With an introductory essay by M.J. Jackson and J. Rogan. SPCK 1962.

Baring-Gould, Sabine, *The Church Revival: Thoughts Thereon and Reminiscences.* Methuen 1914.

———, *The Vicar of Morwenstow: A Life of Robert Stephen Hawker.* Kegan Paul, Trench 1886.

Baskerville, S.W., 'The Political Behaviour of the Cheshire Clergy'. From *Northern History*, vol. xxiii, 1987.

Bateman, Josiah) 'Senex', *Clerical Reminiscences.* Seeley, Jackson & Halliday 1880.

Battiscombe, Georgina, *John Keble: A Study in Limitations.* Constable 1963.

Beeson, Trevor, *The Church of England in Crisis.* Davis-Poynter 1973.

Bell, Alan S., *Sydney Smith.* Oxford: Clarendon Press 1980.

Benson, Arthur Christopher, *The Life of Edward White Benson, Sometime Archbishop of Canterbury.* Two volumes. Macmillan 1899.

Beresford, John (ed.), *The Diary of a Country Parson: The Reverend*

James Woodforde, 1758–1802. Five volumes. Humphrey Milford. Oxford University Press, 1924–31.

Best, G.F.A., *Temporal Pillars: Queen Anne's Bounty, the Ecclesiastical Commissioners, and the Church of England*. Cambridge University Press 1964.

Blomfield, Alfred (ed.), *A Memoir of Charles James Blomfield, D.D. Bishop of London, with Selections from his Correspondence*. John Murray 1863.

Boswell, James, *Life of Dr Samuel Johnson*. Edited by George Birkbeck Hill, revised and enlarged by L.F. Powell. Six volumes Oxford, Clarendon Press 1934.

Braley, Evelyn Foley (ed.), *Letters of Herbert Hensley Henson*. SPCK 1951.

Brose, Olive J., *Church and Parliament: The Reshaping of the Church of England, 1828–1860*. Oxford University Press 1959.

Brown, C.K. Francis, *A History of the English Clergy, 1800–1900* The Faith Press 1953.

Browning, Reed, *The Duke of Newcastle*. New Haven, Conn.: Yale University Press 1975.

Bunting, W.B., *The Parish Church of St Thomas Becket, Chapel-en-le Frith*. Manchester: Sherratt & Hughes 1925.

Campbell, John, Lord, *The Lives of the Lord Chancellors and Keeper of the Great Seal of England, From the Earliest Times till the Reign of King George IV*. Second series, vol. v. John Murray 1846.

Cannon, John, *Aristocratic Century: The Peerage of Eighteenth century England*. Cambridge University Press 1984.

Carpenter, Edward, *Archbishop Fisher: His Life and Times*. Norwich The Canterbury Press 1991.

Carpenter, S.C., *Eighteenth-Century Church and People*. John Murray 1959.

Cash, Arthur H., *Laurence Sterne: The Early and Middle Years* Routledge, 1992 edition.

Chadwick, Owen, *The Victorian Church*. Part two. Adam & Charles Black 1970.

———, *A Victorian Miniature*. Cambridge University Press, 199 edition.

Clive, Mary (ed.), *Caroline Clive: From the Diary and Family Papers of Mrs Archer Clive (1802–1873)*. The Bodley Head 1949.

Collins, Irene, *Jane Austen and the Clergy*. The Hambledon Press 1994.

Colloms, Brenda, *Charles Kingsley: The Lion of Eversley*. Constable 1975.

Coombs, Howard & Peter (eds), *Journal of a Somerset Rector: John Skinner, 1803–1834*. Oxford University Press, 1984 edition.

Cornish, Francis Warre, *A History of the English Church in the Nineteenth Century*. Two volumes. Macmillan 1910.

Crabbe, George, jnr., *The Life of George Crabbe*. Humphrey Milford, Oxford University Press, 1932 edition.

Creighton, Louise, *Life and Letters of Mandell Creighton, Sometime Bishop of London*. Two volumes. Longmans, Green 1904.

(Crockford Prefaces), *The Editor Looks Back*. Geoffrey Cumberlege, Oxford University Press, 1947.

Curtis, Lewis, P., *Chichester Towers*. New Haven, Conn.: Yale University Press 1966.

Davies, G.C.B., *Henry Phillpotts, Bishop of Exeter, 1778–1869*. SPCK, for Church Historical Society, 1954.

De-la-Noy, Michael, *The Church of England: A Portrait*. Simon & Schuster 1993.

Ellman, Edward Boys, *Recollections of a Sussex Parson*. Skeffington 1912.

Evans, Margaret (ed.), *Letters of Richard Radcliffe and John James of Queen's College, Oxford*. Clarendon Press, for Oxford Historical Society, 1888.

Faulkner, Thomas C., with Blair, Rhonda L. (eds), *Selected Letters and Journals of George Crabbe*. Oxford: Clarendon Press 1985.

Ferris, Paul, *The Church of England*. Victor Gollancz 1962.

Galbraith, Georgina (ed.), *The Journal of the Rev. William Bagshaw Stevens*. Oxford: Clarendon Press 1965.

Gascoigne, John, *Cambridge in the Age of the Enlightenment: Science, Religion and Politics from the Restoration to the French Revolution*. Cambridge University Press 1989.

Gatliff, H.E. (ed.), *Stations, Gentlemen!: Memoirs of James Gatliff*. Faber & Faber 1938.

Gisborne, Thomas, *An Enquiry into the Duties of Men in the Higher and Middle Classes of Society in Great Britain, Resulting from their Respective Stations, Professions and Employments*. Two volumes. T. Cadell 1824.

Gore, Charles (ed.), *Essays in Aid of the Reform of the Church*. John Murray 1898.

Graham, Ysenda Maxtone, *The Church Hesitant: A Portrait of the Church of England Today*. Hodder & Stoughton 1993.

Hannah, Gavin (ed.), *The Deserted Village: The Diary of an Oxfordshire Rector, James Newton of Nuneham Courtenay, 1736–86*. Stroud: Alan Sutton 1992.

Hartshorne, Albert (ed.), *Memoirs of a Royal Chaplain, 1729–1763: The Correspondence of Edmund Pyle, D.D., Chaplain in Ordinary to George II, with Samuel Kerrich, D.D., Vicar of Dersingham, Rector of Wolferton, and Rector of West Newton*. John Lane, The Bodley Head 1905.

Haslehurst, R.S.T., 'Victoriana'. From *The Church Quarterly Review*, vol. cxxxii, April–Sept. 1941.

Henson, Herbert Hensley, *Retrospect of an Unimportant Life*, vol. ii. Oxford University Press 1943.

Hinton, Michael, *The Anglican Parochial Clergy: A Celebration*. SCM Press 1994.

Hirschberg, D.R., 'The Government and Church Patronage in England, 1660–1760'. From *Journal of British Studies*, vol. xx, no. 1. Chicago: University of Illinois 1980.

Hunt, Giles, 'A Real-life "Jane Austen Clergyman"'. From *Theology*, vol. lxxix, no. 669, May 1976.

Jacob, W.M., *Lay People and Religion in the Early Eighteenth Century*. Cambridge University Press 1996.

Jukes, H.A. Lloyd (ed.), *Articles of Enquiry Addressed to the Clergy of the Diocese of Oxford at the Primary Visitation of Dr Thomas Secker, 1738*. Banbury: Oxfordshire Record Society 1957.

Ketton-Cremer, R.W., *Country Neighbourhood*. Faber & Faber 1951.

Kirk-Smith, Harold, *William Thomson, Archbishop of York: His Life and Times, 1819–1890*. SPCK, for Church Historical Society, 1958.

Le Faye, Deirdre (ed.), *Reminiscences of Caroline Austen*. Chawton: Jane Austen Society 1986.

Linnell, Charles, *Some East Anglian Clergy*. The Faith Press 1961.

Linnell, C.D. (ed.), *The Diary of Benjamin Rogers, Rector of Carlton, 1720–71*. Streatley: Bedfordshire Historical Record Society 1950.

Linnell, C.L.S. (ed.), *The Diaries of Thomas Wilson, D.D., 1731–37 and 1750. Son of Bishop Wilson of Sodor and Man*. SPCK 1964.

Lock, John, with Dixon, T.W., *A Man of Sorrow: The Life, Letters and Times of the Rev. Patrick Brontë, 1777–1861*. Thomas Nelson 1965.

McClatchey, Diana, *Oxfordshire Clergy, 1777–1869: A Study of the Established Church and the Role of the Clergy in Local Society*. Oxford: Clarendon Press 1960.

MacDonnell, John Cotter, *The Life and Correspondence of William Connor Magee, Archbishop of York, Bishop of Peterborough*. Two volumes. Isbister 1896.

Manwaring, Randle, *From Controversy to Co-existence: Evangelicals in the Church of England, 1914–1980*. Cambridge University Press 1985.

Marsh, Peter T., *The Victorian Church in Decline: Archbishop Tait and the Church of England, 1868–1882*. Routledge & Kegan Paul 1969.

Martin, R.B., *Enter Rumour: Four Early-Victorian Scandals*. Faber & Faber 1962.

Mathieson, William Law, *English Church Reform, 1815–1840*. Longmans, Green 1923.

Mayfield, Guy, *The Church of England: Its Members and Its Business*. Oxford University Press 1958.

Meacham, Standish, *Lord Bishop: The Life of Samuel Wilberforce, 1805–1873*. Cambridge, Mass.: Harvard University Press 1970.

Mitchell, L.G. (ed.), *The Purefoy Letters, 1735–1753*. Sidgwick & Jackson 1973.

Mortlock, C.B., *Inky Blossoms: A Collection of Round-About Papers*. Macdonald & Evans 1949.

Newton, Thomas, *The Life of Dr Thomas Newton, Late Lord Bishop of Bristol*. F.C. & J. Rivington 1816.

Nulle, Stebelton H., *Thomas Pelham-Holles, Duke of Newcastle: His Early Political Career*. Philadelphia: University of Pennsylvania Press 1931.

Obelkevich, James, *Religion and Rural Society: South Lindsey, 1825–1875*. Oxford: Clarendon Press 1976.

Ollard, S.L., and Walker, P.C. (eds), *Archbishop Herring's Visitation Returns, 1743*. Wakefield: Yorkshire Archaeological Society Record Series, vols. lxxi–lxxix, 1928–31.

Palmer, Bernard, *Reverend Rebels: Five Victorian Clerics and Their Fight against Authority*. Darton, Longman & Todd 1993.

Paul, Leslie, *A Church by Daylight: A Reappraisal of the Church of England and its Future*. Geoffrey Chapman 1973.

————, *The Deployment and Payment of the Clergy: A Report*. Church Information Office 1964.

Plomer, William (ed.), *Kilvert's Diary: Selections from the Diary of the Rev. Francis Kilvert, 1 January 1870–13 March 1879*. Three volumes. Jonathan Cape, 1960 edition.

Plumb, J.H., *Sir Robert Walpole*. Two volumes. The Cresset Press 1956, 1960.

Port, M.H., *Six Hundred New Churches: A Study of the Church Building Commission, 1818–1850, and its Church Building Activities*. SPCK, for Church Historical Society, 1961.

Purcell, William, *Onward Christian Soldier: A Life of Sabine Baring-Gould, Parson, Squire, Novelist, Antiquary, 1834–1924*. Longmans, Green 1957.

Roberts, M.J.D., 'Private Patronage and the Church of England, 1800–1900'. From *Journal of Ecclesiastical History*, vol. 32, 1981.

Sandford, E.G. (ed.), *Memoirs of Archbishop (Frederick) Temple by Seven Friends*. Two volumes. Macmillan 1906.

Shaw, Margaret R.B., *Laurence Sterne: The Making of a Humorist, 1713–1762*. The Richards Press 1957.

Smith, Nowell C. (ed.), *Selected Letters of Sydney Smith*. Geoffrey Cumberlege, Oxford University Press, 1956.

Smyth, Charles, *Simeon and Church Order: A Study of the Origins of the Evangelical Revival in Cambridge in the Eighteenth Century*. Cambridge University Press 1940.

Stokes, Francis Griffin (ed.), *The Bletchley Diary of the Rev. William Cole, M.A., F.S.A., 1756–67*. Constable 1931.

Stranks, C.J., *Dean Hook*. A.R. Mowbray 1954.

Sutherland, L.S., with Mitchell, L.G. (eds.), *The History of the University of Oxford: Vol. 5, The Eighteenth Century*. Oxford: Clarendon Press 1986.

Sykes, Norman, *Church and State in England in the Eighteenth Century*. Cambridge University Press 1934.

———, *Edmund Gibson, Bishop of London, 1669–1748: A Study in Politics and Religion in the Eighteenth Century*. Humphrey Milford, Oxford University Press, 1926.

———, 'The Duke of Newcastle as Ecclesiastical Minister'. From *The English Historical Review*, vol. lvii (1942).

Thompson, F.M.L., *English Landed Society in the Nineteenth Century*. Routledge & Kegan Paul 1963.

Thompson, Kennedy A., *Bureaucracy and Church Reform: The Organisational Response of the Church of England to Social Change, 1800–1965*. Oxford: Clarendon Press 1970.

Thomson, A.T. (ed.), *Memoirs of Viscountess Sundon, Mistress of the Robes to Queen Caroline, Consort of George II, Including Letters from the Most Celebrated Persons of her Time*. Two volumes. Henry Colburn 1847.

Thornton, Catherine, with McLaughlin, Frances (eds), *The Fothergills of Ravenstonedale: Their Lives and Their Letters*. William Heinemann 1905.

Trollope, Anthony, *Clergymen of the Church of England*. Reprinted from articles in the *Pall Mall Gazette*. Chapman & Hall 1866.

Verey, David (ed.), *The Diary of a Cotswold Parson*. Gloucester: Alan Sutton 1979.

Virgin, Peter, *The Church in an Age of Negligence: Ecclesiastical Structures and Problems of Church Reform, 1700–1840*. Cambridge: James Clarke 1989.

(Wade, John), *The Extraordinary Black Book: An Exposition of the United Church of England and Ireland … etc., etc.* Effingham Wilson 1831.

Wagner, Anthony, with Dale, Antony, *The Wagners of Brighton*. Phillimore 1983.

Walsh, John, with Haydon, Colin, & Taylor, Stephen (eds.), *The Church of England from c.1689–c.1833: From Toleration to Tractarianism*. Cambridge University Press 1993.

Warne, Arthur, *Church and Society in Eighteenth-Century Devon*. Newton Abbot: David & Charles 1969.

Watson, John Selby, *The Life of William Warburton, D.D., Lord*

Bishop of Gloucester from 1760 to 1799, with Remarks on His Works. Longman, Green, Longman, Roberts, & Green 1863.

Welsby, Paul A., *A History of the Church of England, 1945–1980.* Oxford University Press 1984.

Williams, David, *Genesis & Exodus: A Portrait of the Benson Family.* Hamish Hamilton 1977.

Wingfield-Stratford, Esme, *This Was a Man: The Biography of the Honourable Edward Vesey Bligh, Diplomat-Parson-Squire.* Robert Hale 1949.

Winstanley, D.A., *The University of Cambridge in the Eighteenth Century.* Cambridge University Press 1922.

Wood, R.J., *Leeds Church Patronage in the Eighteenth Century.* Leeds: Publications of Thoresby Society, vol. xli, part 2, 1948.

General reference works

The Chronicle of Convocation (of Canterbury).
The Church Assembly Measures AD 1920–1948.
Hansard's Parliamentary Debates.
Hansard's Parliamentary History of England.

INDEX

217